LEADING WITH A
FOLLOWER'S HEART

Leading,
with a
Follower's
Heart

Eugene B. Habecker

VICTOR BOOKS ®
A DIVISION OF SCRIPTURE PRESS PUBLICATIONS INC.
USA CANADA ENGLAND

Unless otherwise indicated, all Scripture quotations are from the *Holy Bible, New International Version,* © 1973, 1978, 1984, International Bible Society. Used by permission of Zondervan Bible Publishers. Others are from *The Amplified New Testament* (AMP), © 1954, 1958, The Lockman Foundation; and *The Living Bible* (TLB), © 1971, Tyndale House Publishers, Wheaton, IL 60189. Used by permission.

Library of Congress Cataloging-in-Publication Data

Habecker, Eugene B.
   Leading with a follower's heart / by Eugene Habecker.
      p.   cm.
   ISBN 0-89693-769-0
   1. Christian leadership.   I. Title.
BV652.1.H214   1990
253'.2—dc20
                                                      90-31774
                                                          CIP

1 2 3 4 5 6 7 8 9 10 Printing/Year 94 93 92 91 90

CONTENTS

I dedicate this book to my wife Marylou. She and the Lord have taught me the most about leading and following. She continues to help me experience new life and continued growth. It is to her I dedicate the following:

New life—I see it everywhere, from the crying of babies to the growth of new plants. Everywhere, it exists in the physical world. Warm, sensitive, awkward, not smooth, and sometimes unpolished, new life comes to us, a reminder that new beginnings, growth, and change are possible, and essential parts of the rhythm of life.

New life—In Christ. Exhilaration, the excitement of the new believer, the expressions of those newly reborn; freedom from the pain and bondage of sin; forgiveness, freshness, vitality, and vibrancy, all come together in seeming music-like expressions, and giving new harmony and melody to life itself.

New life—Focused not on what once was but on what now is and is to come. Hope, joy, anticipation—all help hide the old, the pain of past failures.

New growth—Helps to cover and remove the scars of bare spots, the wounds of exposed places, bringing healing warmth to the cold, the barrenness of past winters.

New life—Helps me reflect on my helpmate and soulmate, this marvelous gift from God Himself, the giver of all life and of every good and perfect gift. This helpmate, my covenant partner in marriage, equipped by God to be my best earthly friend and healer.

New life—I continue to be given the marvelous gift of new life. I am overwhelmed, humbled, and in awe—indebted to Marylou, God's continuous channel of new life for me.

New life—In Christ, we have new life, a future, and a hope. Today, we celebrate new life. Our hearts and spirits sing of new life. We commit ourselves, now and forever, to new life—for us and for others.

ACKNOWLEDGMENTS

Those who contribute to a book such as this are many and varied. There are several groups of people, however, that deserve special recognition. I note first the many parts of the *Huntington College* community, the students, the staff, the faculty, and the trustees. These various groups, each in their own special way, have taught me more about leading and following than I have yet learned. They have provided continued words of encouragement, many insights, and tangible forms of support, such as manuscript processing and, of great significance, sabbatical leave, which has permitted much of this writing to be completed.

I have appreciated the encouragement and support of the *Regent College* (Vancouver, British Columbia) community, where I have served as a Visiting Scholar in Residence during most of my sabbatical. Regent College is not only located in one of the most beautiful parts of the world, but it is the kind of community of learners which teaches much about *being* the kind of person God desires. I am grateful for Regent's visiting scholar program and for its provision of support space and staff assistance. Regent is blessed with generous people who are always willing to give of themselves and their ideas. You'll see from the book that I frequently refer to several Regent authors.

The *Willingdon Church* in Burnaby, British Columbia and its pastoral staff have contributed much to this project—more than they will ever realize. The Willingdon Church was our "home" church and a source of significant spiritual praise, worship, and nourishment while we were in Canada.

Of particular note are our children, David, Matthew, and Marybeth. It was their willingness to relocate which allowed me the writing and reading time that made this book possible. They have taught and continue to teach me volumes about leading and following.

Finally, Greg Clouse, my editor at Victor Books, has been of considerable help and encouragement during this project. He quietly, yet persistently, kept me on track and on schedule. I have appreciated his many suggestions and helpful additions.

FOREWORD

Along with many others, I was immeasurably helped and challenged by Gene Habecker's earlier book, *The Other Side of Leadership*, which I believe will become a classic in Christian leadership helps. In this second book, which in many ways further develops the themes introduced in his earlier work, my friend Gene—a proven, gifted leader and administrator in his own right—has issued a renewed challenge to us all to recognize and accept the immense responsibility to lead with integrity and follow with diligence.

While much has been written in the field of leadership—both from a Christian and secular perspective—in this incisive volume Habecker has brought together the often-neglected concept that leadership and followership are, in a biblical sense, inextricably linked. We cannot be effective leaders without being followers, first of Christ, and then of those we lead.

God's servants will find in the following pages an array of topics which need to be addressed by the one who wants to effectively serve our Lord Christ—including such vital themes as personal commitment, the use of our spiritual—and natural—gifts, personal renewal, and obedience. Each of the themes is addressed from a scriptural foundation and illustrated in the lives of readily recognizable Bible characters.

Habecker's style of writing is not only candid, attractive, and "full of grace," but he also shares with us eminently practical and biblical principles which can be immediately applied in our daily lives—both as leaders and followers.

He writes most meaningfully about what he refers to as the "inner side of leadership," that rarely dealt with but keenly necessary ingredient that helps us to be the kind of leaders God would have us to be. Externals, obviously, are important, but not nearly as commended by our Lord as those internal values not so readily recognized but at the essence of our lives and character.

In the leadership roles God has allowed me to play, I have long since, and repeatedly, learned that I must follow equally as I am led. The more effective and responsive our followership, the more redemptive our leadership. There are times when as a leader I must follow and times when followers must lead.

Walk through these pages of guidance and wisdom, allow the Holy Spirit to instruct you through them, and I am certain you will find your leadership role increasingly effective, helpful—and evermore enjoyable.

Ted W. Engstrom
President Emeritus
World Vision

In *The Other Side of Leadership* (Victor Books, 1987), I attempted to focus on a variety of items, including an attempt to define leadership, power, and authority. That book had a decided organizational focus. In other words, one of the book's concerns was how we might flesh out the various concepts of leadership in the context of the organization. As such, while the book had a decidedly Christian emphasis and focus, many non-Christians have also found the book to be of some benefit.

Alternatively, the focus of this book is primarily *personal* and addressed to *Christians* who lead and follow in Christian organizations. The focus here includes the quality of one's personal walk with Christ, the "inner side of leading," and the related responsibilities of growing in Christ which that relationship entails. There is a reason for this emphasis.

As I have presented material and ideas from *The Other Side of Leadership* in a variety of seminars and lecture settings, a significant number of questions have been raised and targeted in two primary areas.

First, readers have wondered about the concept of following in leading. As I have discussed this concept throughout North America and in other countries, I sense an overeagerness on the part of leaders to be the boss—the person in charge—and not much eagerness to be the servant or the follower. One writer has indicated his seeming reluctance on this point this way:

> While there is good biblical precedent for keeping the servant perspective, there is no reason to conclude . . . that being a leader means only being a servant and that servants do not command. Managers of households and churches do command.[1]

Second, I have heard many observations and questions that could be properly categorized as pertaining to the spiritual development/formation of the individual leader. This book, then, is addressed to these two primary areas and represents yet another step in my own leadership pilgrimage.

The subject at hand has been pursued along two separate yet complementary routes. The early part of the book focuses primarily on qualitative dimensions and responsibilities of leading and following. In these chapters we explore qualitative issues of the spiritual life such as "commitment," "obedience," "spiritual gifts," "personal renewal," and "spiritual restoration or revival." We'll also focus briefly on some of the considerations involving New Testament leadership requirements for deacons and overseers, examples of early church leaders, and further, the role of the layperson who leads in the local church. At the end of each chapter I have provided "questions for further thought and discussion." These question sections will be particularly focused on how we lead and follow.

The latter part of the book will focus primarily on several role models in the Bible who both led and followed. As you might expect, since I have a particular interest in looking at persons from the perspective of leading *and* following, that bias will be reflected many times in my setting forth the biblical story. I encourage you the reader to both read and study further the context and the content of the entire Scripture passage. I have selected both Old and New Testament examples. Some are personal favorites. All those selected are presumably included in the "great cloud of witnesses" list that appears in Hebrews 12:1:

> Therefore, since we are surrounded by such a great cloud of witnesses, let us throw off everything that hinders and the sin that so easily entangles, and let us run with perseverance the race marked out for us.

These words are not necessarily directed only at leaders, but since most, if not all, of the persons listed performed at some time in their lives important leadership functions, these words seem to me to be particularly applicable for those who lead. Their performance as leaders encourages us in our leading and following.

For example, whenever I think I am faced with a tough leadership assignment, the Spirit of God many times draws me to Hebrews 11 and proceeds to confront me with this kind of question: "All right, carefully review this list. Which of the people listed had an easier leadership assignment than you?" As you might guess, I usually conclude that my assignment has not been nearly as strenuous or demanding as that of those on the list. And then I'm reminded of the incredible sufficiency of God and how He faithfully met their needs. Again, I am persuaded that we can learn much about leading and following by examining how God worked with them in their lives.

I want to make several other observations. First, inasmuch as I see this book in many ways as a companion volume, it would be helpful but not necessary for one's understanding of this book to have first read *The Other Side of Leadership*. This book builds on the framework established by that book, using many of its definitions and assumptions about leadership. Second, if there is a sense that this book reads more easily than *The Other Side of Leadership* and is more devotional in nature, then I have achieved my purpose. Alternatively, you ought not conclude that I distinguish between the sacred and the secular. For I remain firmly persuaded that whatever the Christian brings to God is dedicated to His use and service. As Biehl and Hagelganz have noted, "For Christians there can be no division. All that we do should be considered sacred, whether washing dishes, digging ditches, singing in the sanctuary, watching a play, preaching in the pulpit, talking with a neighbor, saying a prayer, or anything else."[2] Third, while obviously my hope is that you will find this to be a stimulating book, it even more so is intended to encourage and build up leaders and followers in their Christian faith.

Finally, you might reasonably ask, "Why isn't Christ included on your list of leaders who follow?" There are two reasons. In the first place, to place Him on the same list as the others seems to me to devalue who He really is. The Son of God is *the* supreme Leader-Follower. While He took "captivity captive," He also followed His Father all the way to the Cross. In all matters of leading and following, He is our example. All of the other persons mentioned in this book were imperfect. Not so with our Lord. This logically leads to the second reason why Christ is not on the list—Christ as Leader-Follower has been and is the subject of a multitude of additional volumes by others who are better qualified to write those volumes than am I.

With regard to my use of Scripture in this book, in Paul's second letter to Timothy, he makes the following observation: "All Scripture is God-breathed and is useful for teaching, rebuking, correcting, and training in righteousness, so that the man of God may be thoroughly equipped for every good work" (2 Timothy 3:16-17).

It is my strong sense that it is not a violation of the biblical text to suggest that these verses allow for the observation that the leading and following functions are impacted by a wide variety of Scripture. In other words, I don't "buy the argument" that *only* those Scriptures which are presented in a leadership context can be used to discuss qualitative factors in leadership. Coupled with the critically important guidance of the Holy Spirit, the Scripture can be, indeed must be, a critically important part in equipping the leader "for every good work." It is my hope that this book will help continue to move us in that direction.

In my first book I observed that it was not intended to be the final word on the subject of leading and following. Rather, I hoped it would be a good beginning. I have a similar expectation for this book. This book reflects where I am in my efforts at trying to better understand leading and following in the context of an organization. As you'll see, that understanding is far from complete. I have much to learn. I appreciate your willingness to join me in this pilgrimage.

PRELIMINARY OBSERVATIONS ON FOLLOWING AND LEADING

This book emphasizes a special kind of leader, a leader who understands what it means to both lead and follow. From the beginning, I want to note that my idea of "leader" is a broad one and not limited only to "an assigned role or title." In *The Other Side of Leadership*, I identified as leaders those persons who believe "they can and must make a difference in their church, their families, and their communities . . . and . . . to do so following biblical principles." In addition I believe that for the Christian who leads and follows, the ends or objectives aspired to in leadership must also be biblical.

Everywhere I look I see leaders. I see mothers and fathers who each lead in very important and distinctive ways. So too do choir directors, Sunday School teachers, pastors, business executives, faculty, and college and university presidents. I see students who have incredible influence over their peers. Accordingly, I tend to view leadership as being more inclusive than exclusive. Most, if not all, people have a bit of leader in them.

John Kotter makes the distinction between capital "L" leaders (of which there are not very many) and small "l" leaders (of which there are many). He notes that "it would help greatly (in terms of leadership development) if we could get more people to think about leadership in the small 'l' sense. . . ."[1] Unfortunately, many people think about leadership in only the capital "L" sense. Yet both capital "L" and small "l" leaders influence others toward a given end, goal, or purpose, whether the outcomes or objectives be positive or negative. And just as leadership outcomes can be negative or positive, so too can the processes or methods of leading be negative or positive.

POSITIVE AND NEGATIVE LEADING

Here then is a preliminary observation about leadership: it can be positive or negative; it can be slanted toward God's divine purposes or in another direction. It is leadership just the same. Hitler is probably one of the best known examples of a negative leader.

The Scripture is filled with examples of those who led positively. And this book will look at many of them. But the Scripture also contains long lists of those who led negatively, of those who led people away from loving and serving God rather than toward doing so.

Probably one of the better examples of concern for negative leadership in Scripture is found in the Book of Ezekiel. In its own way it illustrates God's desire to have people who are deeply in love with Himself. Nevertheless it stands as a stark reminder that there are consequences for sin and disobedience to a loving Heavenly Father. The writer Ezekiel is graphic in many of his descriptions of the sin of God's people and about His impending judgment on them.

In the first part of chapter 34, Ezekiel communicates the word of the Lord, specifically targeting the shepherds or leaders of Israel, as follows:

> Son of man, prophesy against the shepherds of Israel; prophesy and say to them: "This is what the Sovereign Lord says: Woe to the shepherds of Israel who only take care of themselves! Should not shepherds take care of the flock? You eat the curds, clothe yourselves with the wool and slaughter the choice animals, but you do not take care of the flock. You have not strengthened the weak or healed the sick or bound up the injured. You have not brought back the strays or searched for the lost. You have ruled them harshly and brutally. So they were scattered because there was no shepherd, and when they were scattered they

became food for all the wild animals. My sheep wandered over all the mountains and on every high hill. They were scattered over the whole earth. Therefore, you shepherds, hear the word of the Lord: As surely as I live, declares the Sovereign Lord, because My flock lacks a shepherd and so has been plundered and has become food for all the wild animals, and because My shepherds did not search for My flock but cared for themselves rather than for My flock, therefore, O shepherds, hear the word of the Lord: I am against the shepherds and will hold them accountable for My flock. I will remove them from tending the flock so that the shepherds can no longer feed themselves. I will rescue My flock from their mouths, and it will no longer be food for them" (34:2-10).

Among others, this example of negative leadership identifies at least the following concerns expressed by God about His shepherd leaders of the flock:

First, *the leaders' priority was taking care of themselves and their own needs only rather than expressing care to and taking care of their flocks.* The implication clearly seems to be that the shepherd must have as high a priority taking care of the flock as he has of taking care of himself.

Second, these verses clearly suggest that *there are specific ways in which the leader is supposed to be actively involved with caring for the flock:* strengthening the weak, healing the sick, binding up the weak, bringing back the strays, and searching for those lost sheep. While each of these actions has its contemporary expressions, the idea of the leader caring for the sheep is very powerfully expressed here. Jesus' discussions of the shepherd and sheep in John 10:1-19, Matthew 18:10-14, and elsewhere illustrate the positive example of what a good shepherd does.

Third, *leaders are supposed to lead in specific ways:* "You have ruled over them harshly and brutally" (Ezekiel 34:4). We will see later that leaders are instructed to lead with a quality of gentleness. And however we define gentleness, it clearly seems to me that it doesn't mean "harsh and brutal."

Fourth, *negative leadership has consequences for the flock.* The text notes that because of the poor care of the sheep by the shepherd, the flock wandered and was scattered. The implication is that a good shepherd keeps the flock together.

Fifth, *negative leadership*, not surprisingly, *has negative consequences for the leader:* "I am against the shepherds and will hold them accountable for My flock. I will remove them from tending the flock so that the shepherds can no longer feed themselves" (v. 10).

What really makes our discussion and observation of Christian leadership more difficult is the reality of knowing that we have people in formal or informal leadership roles influencing others toward ends and objectives which are not necessarily biblical. And if "the people being led" are biblically illiterate, that is, if they're not "examining the Scriptures every day to see if what the leader said is true" (Acts 17:11, my paraphrase), the followers are more capable of being misled by these Christian leaders.

It seems clear that *what* the Christian leader aspires to in leadership in the context of the Christian organization must reflect biblical objectives and purposes. Further, *how* one leads must reflect biblical processes and ways of dealing with people. And the motives or the *why* of leading which infect one's leadership must also be proper, reflecting biblical qualities.

FOLLOWING AND LEADING

With regard to leadership, and as I observed at some length in my previous book, I view leading and following as inextricable parts of the same whole. Arguably, one cannot be a leader without having followers. I define a follower as being somewhat different than a subordinate. I view a subordinate as a person who under the direction of a superior carries out some kind of assigned role or responsibility. The subordinate can carry out this role or responsibility with great joy and eagerness or with great reluctance and a sense of "have to." When I carry out my responsibility or role because *I want to* rather than because *I have to*, I move in the direction of being a follower. It seems to me that Christ wanted followers, not subordinates.

One of the great mistakes made by some leaders is their tendency to see "followers" as having little if any capacity to influence the direction of either the "problems" or the "opportunities" faced by organizations. Such leaders see themselves as the primary fountain of organizational truth and corporate enlightenment. Woe to any subordinate who "crosses" this kind of leader.

Robert Kelley discusses this kind of leader this way: "We tend to think of followers as passive sheep." But, says Kelley, "Effective followers do question the judgment of leaders and compare their sense of what's right and wrong against what's asked of them."[2] I want to state Kelley's point even more strongly: Effective followers *must* question the judgment of leaders. To be sure, leaders do have insights about the organization and its vision. But so too do followers. An effective leader celebrates the "we-ness" not the "my-ness" of an organization's accomplishments. An effective leader celebrates "the team as hero."

In the same way that subordinates can have the attitude of a follower, so too must a leader. When leaders subordinate their ideas and plans to the review and input of their followers, when leaders learn from followers, when leaders are strongly committed to the welfare of their followers, when leaders do all of this while still moving people forward to the implementation of the proper goals and mission of the unit they lead, and when they do all of this with a sense of great joy and delight in service to others, leaders in some way have become followers. And as a result of input from followers, actions by leaders can be improved and made better. This is a role that effective leaders must constantly play.

One illustration of followership, particularly in the context of the local church, is the following:

> All . . . should anticipate the day when the laity will rise up and say to their appointed clergy, "We welcome you here to our congregation and look forward to your leadership among us. But realizing that you will be with us for only a while, we will tell you the story of our church. We will identify for you the aspects of this church that make us love it, the crises we have endured, and our dreams for the future. We will listen to your dreams and your insights about how we might be more faithful, but first you must respect what God has done here among us."[3]

While traditions and processes for pastoral selection and appointment differ, this sense of ongoing pastoral openness to the people—whether expressed by all the people, a representative board, or through other ways—helps us better understand what I mean by "follower." I see this followership element to be part of and essential to effective leadership of any kind.

This willingness to follow, it seems to me, was marvelously demonstrated by Christ in so many ways. Paul sets it forth eloquently in Philippians 2:5-8:

> Your attitude should be the same as that of Christ Jesus: who being in very nature God, did not consider equality with God something to be grasped, but made Himself nothing, taking the very nature of a servant, being made in human likeness. And being found in appearance as a man, He humbled Himself and became obedient to death—even death on a cross.

As a Christian, therefore, I can't be an effective leader without also being a follower, a follower first of all of Christ, and secondly, of the people I lead. As Calvin Miller has observed: "Every Christian who desires to become a leader must *first* know how to follow" (emphasis mine).[4] It's what Henri Nouwen calls a leader's "willingness to be led."[5] Again, I am convinced that I will be effective in leading only as I faithfully submit all of my leadership responsibilities (and the way I carry them out) to the teaching of what it means to be an obedient follower of Jesus Christ *and* only as I seek to be sensitive to and follow the input from the people I lead.

Further, I am persuaded that seeking input from and being sensitive to the people I lead does not necessarily mean that I have abandoned an assigned leadership responsibility. There are those who argue that being sensitive to the people in this followership role means that I have given up my leadership role to the people. And as a result the organization stagnates, ceases to exist, or if it does, serves no useful purpose. As I stated in my previous book, an effective leader, even though a servant of the people, nevertheless must help keep people moving along or toward a given course or direction. The shepherd, for example, doesn't serve the sheep well if the flock is permitted to move randomly in all directions at will. I like how Gardner expresses this: "The leader/follower relationship is at best mutually nourishing, mutually strengthening. It is not a bland relationship. It is not without tension and conflict. . . . The ideal is leadership strong enough to propose clear directions and followers strong enough to criticize and amend—and finally, enough continuity of purpose to resolve disputes and move on."[6]

Accordingly, there are times when leaders must follow and times when followers must lead. An effective leader must wear both hats, so to speak. As an article in the *Harvard Business Review* points out, "Followership is not a person but a role, and what distinguishes followers from leaders is not intelligence or character but the role they play. . . . Effective followers and effective leaders are often the same people playing different parts at different parts of the day."[7] So rather than discussing only leadership, my preference is to talk about and discuss the leader-follower and leading and following.

Here then is an important distinction I want to make as we proceed: *Whenever I talk about leaders throughout the course of this book, I do so in the context of the leader as being one who follows and leads. Whenever I discuss followers, I mean a follower who both leads and follows.*

In the same way that one can't be an effective Christian without being a faithful follower of Christ, so too I am convinced that an organization will not be able to achieve its optimal potential without somebody in the organization encouraging and enabling each person therein to develop and enhance both followership and leadership roles. So while I have a concern about leadership, I have an equal concern for the role of the follower.

In my work in Christian higher education, I am hired by a board of trustees. I need to follow their policies. But there are times when I must (and they desire me to) give leadership to the board, even though I am not a board member. I have a responsibility to lead the faculty. Yet the truth is that they know far more than I do in a variety of areas, particularly in their given curricula. So in that role I also need to be a follower and learner. I need to provide leadership for students; yet I must be attentive to their concerns, listening to their needs and the expressions of their desires as to how to make the college better for them. In that role I follow. I provide leadership for an administrative team, yet they are experts in the areas in which they provide leadership. So therefore I must follow their lead in many matters. I could give many additional examples about my involvement in the local church, the community, and the home.

Again, one of the greatest mistakes made by leaders is for them to view themselves and to permit others to see them as the "only" leader and everyone else in the organization as the followers. Such an arrangement unduly and unnecessarily burdens the leader and limits the probability that the organization will achieve its goals. At the same time, this limited view of leadership seems to suggest to the followers that they (the followers) have no concern for the welfare of the organization. Yet the reality remains that neither the organization nor the individuals within it will achieve their potential unless each recognizes the need for active participation (as leaders and followers) in the life, work, and ministry of the organization. As Birnbaum has stated, "It should come as no surprise that leaders are as dependent on constituencies (followers) as constituencies (followers) are on leaders."[8] And as Moss-Kanter has observed: "There are not enough creative geniuses to go around and there are too many problems ... in this era for them to afford to have only a handful of people thinking about solutions."[9]

Perhaps our most powerful example of "followership" comes from the concept of biblical giftedness in members of the body of Christ as evidenced in the local church. Whether dealing with 1 Corinthians 12, 1 Peter 4, Romans 12, or other passages, the sense communicated is that each person who is a member of the body of Christ has at least one gift and is therefore *necessary* for that body if the body is to properly function. And the "leader" of the local church who ignores utilizing each gift and each member of that body will probably not see the full potential of that body reached. Just as the physical body does not function properly if the more prominent members of that body do not permit each member to take the lead in an assigned role, so too with the body of Christ. Paul hammers this home with great force in 1 Corinthians 12:12-31.

It is important for me to observe in this discussion about followership that the CEO-type in an organization, even though fully committed to the operative concept of followership, may still carry the ultimate operating authority (legally) for the organization. In many North American organizations, the ultimate responsibility for organization policy rests legally and officially with a board of directors or trustees. After issues have been discussed, debated, and argued; after facts have been presented and analyzed; there usually are recommendations/options that emerge and decisions that need to be made and pursued. The difficulty comes not from the process of confirming as "final" those recommendations that are clearly supported by all, including the leader. Rather, the difficulty arises from the divided house of substantial disagreement. Here is where the people, including the leader, have to be particularly sensitive to the Holy Spirit's leading. In the absence of a clear recommendation or sense of how to proceed, and assuming that a decision must be made "now," the ultimate decision falls to the one accountable to lead. Given my commitment to followership and to process, I don't relish those opportunities. Yet that too is an important and necessary part of leadership.

PERSONAL AND ORGANIZATIONAL LEADERSHIP

One of the difficulties of having an inclusive definition of leadership is that it tends to overlook the unique needs and expectations of organizational leadership. By organizational leadership I'm talking about an entity that is voluntarily brought into existence by a group of people to achieve a given purpose or need, and which usually tends to be incorporated legally. Christian colleges, mission agencies, parachurch organizations, and an "organized local church" (as compared with *the* church) tend to be the kinds of organizations I'm referring to.

When we discuss personal leadership as influence, we appropriately move to broader considerations of leading and following. As I have previously noted, leaders and followers are all around us. These are the leaders who may or may not have a real or perceived formal leadership title or role, yet who have wide influence. They may or may not be part of an organization. Parents are one example. Book authors, teachers, and newspaper columnists are still others. I believe, for example, that leaders teach and that teachers lead. I was reminded of this anew during a recent trip to Australia.

While there I was challenged in my thinking about leadership by an article in an Australian magazine[10] entitled "What Makes a Great Teacher?" I was intrigued because many of the qualities listed for great teachers also apply to leaders. Ranked in priority order, key *qualities* were as follows: be able to enthuse students; treat them as individuals; know the subject; be loving and warm; teach to learn; empathize with students; relate to others; be firm, fair, and flexible; be organized; prepare students for life; manage the classroom; have high self-esteem; have a sense of humor; be a complete person; and take risks.[11] Almost without exception, these are also qualities of great leaders. And if I were to ask the question, "What are qualities of great mothers, fathers, pastors, or a variety of other roles?" many if not all of these qualities would be on that list.

But are there differences in leadership with regard to the situation in which leadership is being exercised? Does the person who primarily spends his or her time in an office writing on a text processer, and whose leadership influence comes primarily through books and articles, possess leadership skills in the same way as the leader who directs an organization with several hundred personnel (paid and volunteer) and a $50 million budget? Asked a different way, what are some of the distinctives or tendencies of organizational leadership? While similarities are many, I believe there are some differences between personal and organizational leadership. I want to suggest several.

First, *organizational leadership has a primary focus on interacting with people within the organization.* In an organization, one *must* practice leading and following. Whether with family or company personnel, the leader of an organization has as a primary mandate the development and care of people.

Second, *organizational leadership has a commitment to achieve a purpose or mission.* Organizations are brought into existence not just to exist but with a goal in mind. For example, students are educated; the hungry are fed; and missionaries are sent to the field to share their faith. Further, non-volunteer personnel expect to be paid for their services at regular time periods. So however good might be the leader's skills at getting along with people, however personable he or she might be, these other organizational ends need to be met as well. Further, actions taken and policies developed must reflect consistency with biblical means and ends.

Given the need to achieve a mission, there is often tension between competing means and methods needed to achieve it. Problems result where a leader has followers but where the mission is not being achieved or moved toward. I say this knowing that there are always situations where "success" escapes many organizations and yet God's presence and direction are evident. The opposite is also true. These situations, however, provide opportunities for useful reexamination of an organization's purposes and mission. I'm not convinced that it is always God's will that once called into existence, an organization is "ordained by God" to be around forever. It's tough to ascertain God's will in these matters, particularly given our human tendencies to grow and expand. What "leader" wants to be known by others as the one who closed down an "organization"?

Third, in organizational leadership, *one's call to leadership must be confirmed by followers in an ongoing fashion.* Few persons who hold positions of authority will see subordinates become followers if in fact the people refuse to confirm one's leadership. Examples abound in both secular and Christian organizations where this confirmation did not take place. Further, this confirmation must be ongoing for leadership to be effective. The fact that I begin my leadership assignment to the usual fanfare and accolades of followers is no guarantee that it will continue.

Just how long should I stay in a position of organizational leadership? Obviously, I can't answer that question for you. But I believe it is an issue that needs some discussion.[12] Certainly, movement toward the achievement of an organization's mission, assuming proper methods are being used to do so, may be an indication of effective leadership. Further, I believe the followers must continually be confirming the leadership of the leader. That doesn't mean, of course, that followers will always agree with or like the decisions ultimately made. And it certainly doesn't mean that the leader should be making decisions based on the sole criterion, "I want to be liked by the followers." But there should be broad support for the leader throughout the organization.

Fourth, *the organizational leader has to guard against becoming consumed by the needs and burdens of the organization.*[13] While there are burdens to be sure in personal leadership, they are intense in organizational leadership. There are the burdens of personnel decisions. There are the burdens of finance—making sure bills are paid and paychecks issued on time. Knowing that hundreds of families are depending on the "right decision" is of significant consequence to the leader. And then there are the burdens related to the mission of the organization. Seeing starving children around the world every week takes its own toll. Few leaders relish carrying these kinds of burdens, yet most know the realities of doing so. The Apostle Paul enumerated the kinds of burdens he carried in 2 Corinthians 11, noting in verse 28 that "besides everything else, I face daily the pressure of my concern for the churches."

Some of Christ's most encouraging and comforting words for leaders and followers are found in Matthew 11:28-30:

> Come to Me, all you who are weary and burdened, and I will give you rest. Take My yoke upon you and learn from Me, for I am gentle and humble in heart and you will find rest for your souls. For My yoke is easy and My burden is light.

Jesus Christ gives rest to all of the burdened and weary. As we take on His yoke (way) and as He teaches us, we find inner rest for our souls. His yoke is easy and His burden is light. What refreshing news and comfort for leaders and followers. These words make it easier to be His follower *and* His leader.

QUESTIONS FOR FURTHER THOUGHT AND DISCUSSION

1. Identify the people you know who you say are leaders, even though they hold no position of "formal" leadership. Why did you identify them? What qualities do they possess?
2. If you could choose to exercise influence through an informal role or through a formal role, which would you choose and why? Can you think of ways in which your effectiveness as a leader might be enhanced because you don't hold a formal position of leadership?
3. Do you think Kotter's distinction between capital "L" and small "l" leaders is a useful one? Why or why not?
4. Do you agree or disagree with the idea that an organization, once founded, should stay in existence permanently? On what basis would you recommend that an organization be continued or discontinued?

SPIRITUAL QUALIFICATIONS FOR LEADERS

Qualifications for positions of leadership within Christian organizations at first glance seem to be pretty straightforward. Usually applicants are expected to be persons of Christian commitment. Once that has been determined, then the inquiry moves into the more traditional areas such as educational qualifications, appropriate experience, and organizational fit. Local churches often expect that "leaders" be active "members" of the church organization as well.

Both the Old and New Testaments discuss at some length qualifications for holding positions of leadership, though there is a tendency to consider them many times in only a perfunctory way. After all, what does the Scripture know about contemporary management and leadership expectations? How can a book about religion speak to the many dilemmas which must be handled to survive the typical management jungle?

THE OLD TESTAMENT AND LEADERSHIP

While it may be easy for us to identify with the spiritual, moral, and ethical dimensions faced by the many leaders identified and discussed in the Scripture, particularly those in the Old Testament, we tend to forget that these same people regularly handled and managed hundreds of millions if not billions of dollars in revenues and expenditures. In addition, many regularly managed and directed hundreds of thousands of people. In other words, if the scenarios which come to us from the pages of biblical history were presented to us in contemporary "Fortune 500" fashion as the megabusinesses they in fact were, perhaps we would be inclined to take them more seriously.

What also makes such a discussion difficult for us is that in most of the examples which we will cite the choice of leader was God-directed. And given the Lord's ability to look beyond surface responses into the innermost parts of a person, coupled with His ability to know future performance capacity, the quality of the person selected was never in doubt. On the other hand, given our human inabilities and our limited knowledge, our selections tend to include a greater capacity for error.

Nevertheless, it seems that we can learn from biblical examples, particularly so when we focus on the qualities of character exhibited by those ultimately selected. While we might lament our finite selection capacities, we must remember that we too can depend on the leadership of the Holy Spirit in these matters, who, Jesus said, "will teach you all things and will remind you of everything I have said to you" (John 14:26). Presumably this also applies to our selection of leaders. Accordingly, we must learn here to recognize the potential of our ignorance or limitations.

A sense of arbitrariness sometimes seems to characterize the leadership selections of the Old Testament. Obviously God can select whomever He desires to provide leadership; after all, He is God. We are but clay and He is the potter.

There is a sense, nevertheless, that a person's walk with God is always seen as indispensable for a leadership assignment. For example, note the observation about Noah, God's choice to be the preserver of the human race from the Flood: "Noah was a righteous man, blameless among the people of his time, and he walked with God" (Genesis 6:9). While we don't know whether or not Noah was the only one who fulfilled these qualities, we can perhaps assume that Noah's selection was based in part on his willingness to "walk with God." And then there's Abraham. We're not given the reason in Genesis 12 why God selected Abraham to be the one who would become the father of a great nation. But given the very positive relationship we witness between God and Abraham, we know that he either was a godly person when he was selected or at least became a very godly man after his selection.

There are numerous other examples which suggest that spiritual fitness and vitality are prime ingredients for leadership. Yet it is difficult to make the generalization that God always and only selected known godly people to carry out a leadership assignment. We don't know much about the initial spiritual condition of persons such as Gideon, Saul, or Aaron, yet God saw fit to use them in leadership roles. What additionally complicates our efforts is that particularly in the Old Testament, we also see some leadership assignments granted on the basis of family heritage. Following the family lines of Abraham, David, and the clan of Levi illustrates this. In the New Testament we even see a person selected for the important leadership role of apostle by drawing lots (Acts 1:24-26).

Paradoxically, there seem to be instances when God, in order to achieve a God-directed end, selected persons who were not necessarily known for their godliness to carry out His plans and purposes. This was particularly the case when God used an enemy of Israel to bring judgment on them. Examples here would include persons such as Nebuchadnezzar (see Jeremiah 27) and Cyrus, Darius, and Artaxerxes (see Ezra and Nehemiah).

In brief, the record of the Old Testament is filled with those chosen as leaders at God's own discretion. The message given by God to Jeremiah illustrates this point: "With My great power and outstretched arm I made the earth and its people and the animals that are on it, and *I give it to anyone I please*" (Jeremiah 27:5, emphasis mine).

So, just what are some Old Testament qualifications for leadership?

1. *God looks for leaders who have hearts perfect toward Him.* As a general observation (and there are other examples to the contrary), the God of the Old Testament seems to be preoccupied with finding persons whose hearts are perfect toward Him. Furthermore, His search in that direction appears to be continuous, though it does not always culminate with success. Note the following:

For the eyes of the Lord range throughout the earth to strengthen those whose hearts are fully committed to Him (2 Chronicles 16:9).

The Lord looks down from heaven on the sons of men to see if there are any who understand, any who seek God (Psalm 14:2).

I looked for a man among them who would build up the wall and stand before Me in the gap on behalf of the land so I would not have to destroy it, but I found none (Ezekiel 22:30).

2. *God looks for leaders of great inner spiritual stature.* If it is true, and I believe it is, that God desires godly people to carry on the work He calls people to do, it also appears to be true that He is unimpressed with the physical appearances of those He selects to be leaders. Further, He does not appear to be impressed with one's pedigree, formal education, or prior leadership experience. He goes way beyond all of that to the thoughts and intents of the heart. Again, note the following:

The Lord has sought out a man after His own heart and appointed him leader of His people, because you have not kept the Lord's command (1 Samuel 13:14).

But the Lord said to Samuel, "Do not consider his appearance or his height, for I have rejected him. The Lord does not look at the things man looks at. Man looks at the outward appearance, but the Lord looks at the heart" (1 Samuel 16:7, speaking about David's older brother Eliab).

For the Lord searches every heart and understands every motive behind the thoughts (1 Chronicles 28:9).

From heaven the Lord looks down and sees all mankind; from His dwelling place He watches all who live on earth— He who forms the hearts of all, who considers everything they do (Psalm 33:13-15).

From these Scriptures and others, the most desired quality of character appears to be the inner self, dedicated and fully committed to the Lord. As a colleague recently observed, "As leaders, our primary obligation is to become more Christlike. After all, one ministers and leads out of what one is."

3. *What God expects of leaders He also desires for all of us.* Let me give several examples.

☐ When King David asks the questions—"Lord, who may dwell in Your sanctuary? Who may live on Your holy hill?" (Psalm 15:1)—the admonition to blameless living, truthful speech, and honest relationships appears to apply to all, not just leaders.

☐ When Moses gets to the bottom line of his account of how he received the Ten Commandments from God, he likewise admonishes both leaders and followers: "And now, O Israel, what does the Lord your God ask of you but to fear the Lord your God, to walk in all His ways, to love Him, to serve the Lord your God with all your heart and all your soul, and to observe the Lord's commands and decrees that I am giving you today for your own good" (Deuteronomy 10:12-13).

☐ When the Prophet Micah asks the big question—"And what does the Lord require of you?"—his answer applies universally: "To act justly and to love mercy and to walk humbly with your God" (Micah 6:8).

When I begin to understand that the clear teachings of Scripture apply to all who name the name of Christ, not just leaders *or* followers but leaders *and* followers, then I begin to understand and recognize the enabling and empowering role that I play as a leader. But just as importantly, it makes me more open to understanding all the things I can learn in my role as follower. Further, it provides by implication a mandate to all the people in the organization to understand that their contributions of leadership to the organization are vital if its mission and purposes are to be achieved. Again, here is where the concept of followership makes incredible sense.

It doesn't appear that God selects leaders and then cares not one wit about the spiritual makeup of the rest of the people. Somehow we have to get away from the idea that leaders are somehow more special and privileged in the eyes of God than those being led. (Yes, I am well aware of 1 Timothy 5:17.) Each individual has leading and following roles that need to be carried out. Therefore the CEO has to make sure "followers" don't wallow in the myth that the "leader" is somehow better than they are.

I have been to numerous commissioning services, whether for missionary service, pastoral service, or other leadership roles. The sense communicated at many tends to run along these lines: You are part of God's elite; you are worthy of special honor; and you will be specially blessed of God. To be sure, leaders do influence people but people also influence leaders. It is God's desire that *all* who name the name of Christ should grow in maturity.

THE NEW TESTAMENT AND LEADERSHIP

As with the Old Testament, the New Testament, particularly the Gospels, contains a variety of references as to how a leader ought to function in community. For instance, Jesus' clear teaching in Matthew (especially chapters 5–7) is full of more spiritual meat and instruction than most of us can even hope to master in a lifetime. The parables and other teachings of Christ throughout all of the Gospels likewise are storehouses of profound truth. The way Christ worked with people illustrates tremendous insight as to how we can be responsive to people and meet their needs. The methods He used to deal with government officials and those who claimed to be the proper religious authorities illustrate a variety of truth, including differences between political expediency and righteous action, and the proper roles and domains of a human political government in contrast with the kingdom of God.

As with the Old Testament, these teachings of Christ do not appear to be targeted or limited in any special way to leaders. As a matter of fact, Christ seemingly has words of caution for those either aspiring to be leaders or those already functioning as leaders, such as:

- [ ] Don't seek to be first;
- [ ] Prefer others;
- [ ] Don't lord your leadership over others.

Many times we are tempted to view the teachings of Christ as applying only to one's personal life, in isolation from one's organizational life. It's as if Christians in organizations read and understand the principles of Scripture but, in the practices of the organization, we simply don't see how these principles apply. Accordingly, they aren't followed.

Why is it, for example, that persons who preach obedience to the commands of Christ Sunday after Sunday practice almost daily the raw exercise of secular power in other aspects of the church's organizational life, seeking always to be first and making sure that they hold the absolute power within the church? Why is it that well-intentioned evangelical Christians who have degrees in theology and who hold positions of leadership preside over Christian organizations which, in some cases, follow practices and procedures that are clearly unbiblical? Why is it that at some of the better-known evangelical organizations (including churches, seminaries, and colleges) in North America, the leader is referred to as "dictator" behind his back; where he insists on all of the perquisites of office that his secular counterparts do; and where the people know it is not in their best interest to "cross the boss"?

Rebecca Pippert gives an example of an international businessman who illustrates the concern I have in mind:

> I am on two boards. One is with a religious organization, and the other is with secular people. With the secular board members, I know that many are out for their own agenda. They manipulate and control and deceive. I know it, and so do they. But frankly, I've seen lots of the same controlling, manipulative, deceitful behavior on the religious board. The difference is not the behavior but in the fact that the secular board members often acknowledge their motives, whereas the believers don't. The believers not only deny them, but cover their motives with pious words. They talk spiritually, but they are playing the same game.[1]

It is for these reasons that our focus in leading must be on hearing *and* doing the Word of God. As James puts it quite clearly, "Do not merely listen to the Word, and so deceive yourselves. Do what it says" (James 1:22).

While it does appear that the principles and teachings of the New Testament apply to all believers, including leaders, there are, nevertheless, several prominent lists of stated qualifications for leaders, particularly church leaders. In particular, I refer to those that Paul wrote about in 1 Timothy 3 and in Titus 1.

PRELIMINARY OBSERVATIONS
ABOUT "THE LISTS"

Before we talk briefly about the things that Paul thought essential to particular roles in church leadership, we probably should make several preliminary observations about them. First, the lists are not necessarily presented as inclusive. In other words, other scriptural commands not included in this list cannot be ignored because they are absent. Just because the subject of love is not addressed here (as it is, for example, in 1 Corinthians 13) does not give us license to be unloving. So too with the teaching about the fruit of the Spirit (Galatians 5). Second, this list says next to nothing about *how* these leaders were to be selected. Perhaps the selection process was to be democratic, perhaps by lot, perhaps by appointment. But whatever the process, Paul seems to be saying that at a minimum those selected needed to possess the personal qualities of character and conduct so listed. Third, the list does not contain a job description for leaders. Perhaps there is an assumption here that what a leader does, and how that is done, will be influenced by the character of the leader. Fourth, the list presented appears to include items which stood in contrast to the practices of the world culture in which these leaders would operate. It is as if Paul were saying, "Compared with the practices of the pagan world in which you will find yourselves, I want you to be people of unquestioned character who operate under a different code of conduct."

While we need to exercise great care as to the conclusions drawn from what Paul did not include on his list, several observers have noted that to Paul it didn't particularly matter *how* one was chosen or *what* one would do in the job role. What was of paramount concern to Paul was the character and the conduct of the one chosen. It is almost as if Paul were saying, "If the person's conduct is proper and if one's character is above reproach, you will get a good leader." As one writer has observed:

> In preaching to outsiders, in maintaining the betterness of the gospel, in winning converts and establishing believers, it will be conduct, not creed, character, not controversy, practice, not precept, that will play the weightier part.[2]

All of this seems strangely familiar to some of the Old Testament examples mentioned earlier. What God wanted (and still wants) are people who have hearts perfect toward Him. He may choose to use others but this appears to be His strong desire and overriding preference.

PAUL'S QUALIFICATIONS FOR THE LEADER

The lists of leadership expectations found in 1 Timothy 3 and Titus 1 are well worth reviewing. In these two important passages Paul generally discusses the qualifications for both elders/overseers and deacons. These roles tend to be similar yet different in the New Testament. Some, for example, suggest that the role of *deacon* slants in the direction of those responsibilities identified in Acts 6:2, while the role of *elder* slants in the direction of those responsibilities identified in Acts 6:4. For purposes of this discussion, we will discuss primarily Paul's list from 1 Timothy 3. Further, since many similarities exist between the qualifications listed here for elders/overseers and deacons, we'll handle them together.

1. *Above reproach and respectable* (verses 2, 8). It appears to be Paul's sense that candidates for this position needed to be persons about whom people would not be able to find fault. And this clean record, so to speak, could not be one of recent standing. The record had to be clean over the long haul.

Does this requirement suggest that only perfect people from birth can hold these types of positions? Obviously not, as Paul himself (and Moses and others) failed to honor Christ in all that he did until later in life. What it does appear to mean is that the person considered for this type of leadership position ought to be one who is mature yet still growing in the faith, who understands both God's grace and His forgiveness, and who is seen by the people being led as having a reputation worthy of respect. Perhaps one of the reasons for this requirement is to make sure that the leader never becomes the issue in leadership.

When I was active in organized athletics, every game I ever participated in had "officials" or referees. One of the things our coach always said to us before a game was never to let the referee become the issue in a game. In fact, it was his contention that a good referee seldom became the issue in a game. What he meant by that was that a good official tried to make such fair and consistent calls that the players never lamented or celebrated them. In that way attention could be properly centered on the game and its progress. Interestingly, if the referee had a "bad" reputation, we players were more unforgiving of his bad calls than if he came to the game with a good reputation.

So too for the leader. If the leader is above reproach, it is more likely that people will better focus their collective energies on the needs, goals, and purposes of the organization and its people rather than on the leader. All of us have witnessed situations where the organization did not move forward because its leadership was *under* a cloud rather than *above* reproach.

This "above reproach" expectation is probably one reason why a "larger" rather than "smaller" group ought to be involved in the leadership selection process. While the conclusion "above reproach" can be made by one person, the idea here is that this conclusion would carry more weight if such reflected the judgments of "more" rather than "fewer" godly people.

2. *Husband of one wife* (verses 2, 12). Is this a statement directed at those who wanted to practice polygamy? Is it targeted to those previously married, divorced, and subsequently remarried? Paul was generally opposed to divorce (1 Corinthians 7:11-12) and elsewhere he had written that "each man should have his own wife" (1 Corinthians 7:2), a statement that illustrates his disdain for the polygamy that was regularly practiced in that culture. It seems to be clear, therefore, that Paul's concern was that church leaders are to have but one wife.

3. *Temperate and self-controlled* (verse 2). These two appear to be related. Someone who is temperate is someone not given to wild extremes. This speaks to me about having an evenness to the way one lives and approaches life, not being subject to repeated highs and lows. Is Paul, therefore, suggesting that a person should be unemotional, never showing anger, never reflecting bitter disappointment and emotional upset over the loss of a loved one,

never given to deep despair? Probably not. Alternatively, he couples the need to be temperate with self-control. Obviously one does this (and perhaps can only do this) through the strength of Christ Himself (Galatians 2:20).

Paul in numerous places talks about the importance of self-control in the Christian walk. For example, in Galatians 5 he lists it as part of the fruit of the Spirit: "But the fruit of the Spirit is love, joy, peace, patience, kindness, goodness, faithfulness, gentleness, and self-control" (Galatians 5:22-23). He repeatedly discusses the importance of self-control in the Book of Titus (cf. 1:8; 2:2, 5-6, 12).

What Paul seems to be saying is that one of the character qualities of a believer is self-control. And this is particularly true for leaders. Accordingly, as a leader, I am called upon to exercise restraint and to be temperate, to demonstrate an evenness in all of life and to be under control in how I approach my leadership responsibilities. Can my conduct reflect frequent outbursts of rage? Probably not.

4. *Hospitable* (verse 2). The dictionary defines this term as "giving, disposed to give, welcome and entertainment to strangers or guests." Both Paul and Peter encouraged this. Paul exhorted us to: "Share with God's people who are in need. Practice hospitality" (Romans 12:13). Peter said it this way: "Offer hospitality to one another without grumbling" (1 Peter 4:9).

In the daily leadership grind, when people work long, tiring, and stressful hours, and look forward to home as one's place of security and refreshment, this expectation to be hospitable often gets lost by the wayside. Yet Paul stated this as an expectation of leadership. Perhaps one of the reasons both Peter and Paul identify this as an expectation for all believers, especially leaders, is because they both benefited and experienced refreshment from those skilled with the gift of hospitality.

5. *Able to teach/teachable* (verse 2). An effective leader must reflect both a teachable spirit in how matters are handled and be able to teach well. One who possesses a teachable spirit will be a better learner. Paul also intended for these church leaders to be good teachers of the Word of God. Perhaps he had this in mind when he said to

Timothy: "Do your best to present yourself to God as one approved, a workman who . . . correctly handles the word of truth" (2 Timothy 2:15). Interestingly, the literature on leadership underscores the fact that one leads by and through what one teaches. Alternatively, people also teach by and how they lead. Good leaders teach and great teachers lead.

6. *Not given to much wine* (verses 3, 8). While other Scriptures, particularly Old Testament ones, speak to the issue of abstinence, this is not one of them. While personally I'd prefer this verse to read, "Not given to wine," that's not the text. While Paul does not insist on abstinence as a requirement for leadership, he is careful to identify only wine, not beer (Proverbs 31:4) or other fermented drink (Leviticus 10:9) as permissible. Further, he notes that even in one's use of wine, one must exercise restraint and self-control, including its nonuse if to do so would cause a brother to fall (Romans 14:21).

My observations of Christian leaders for more than two decades suggest that many take great liberty with this verse, using it to justify the use and consumption of a wide variety of alcoholic beverages. Many do so not out of genuine enjoyment of the beverage but rather because of a conviction that they'll be better liked and more accepted by non-Christians. There's almost a sense that only those who are unenlightened would choose to abstain from the use of alcoholic beverages in moderation. While Paul's statement clearly allows for the use of wine in moderation, he also had previously stated that the leader's life was to reflect practices which were above reproach. Again, given society's tremendous problems with alcohol abuse, voluntary abstinence may best preserve the reputation and influence of the leader in these matters.

7. *Not violent but gentle, not quarrelsome* (verse 3). Again, part of the fruit of the Spirit is peace and gentleness. Elsewhere in the Epistles Paul cautions against divisiveness, complaining, and arguing; for example, "The Lord's servant must not quarrel; instead he must be kind to everyone" (2 Timothy 2:24). The writer of the Proverbs tells us that a gentle answer turns away wrath (Proverbs 15:1). Peter tells us that in giving others an answer about our

faith we are to do so with gentleness and respect (1 Peter 3:15-16). Effective leaders are called upon and expected to be gentle and peaceable.

Following this list of *qualities of character* that are expected of leaders, Paul turns next to two other potential areas of concern—family and money.

8. *Proper management of family and obedient children* (verses 4, 12). Candidates for positions of leadership are typically asked questions having to do with prior experience in organizational leadership situations, but how often are they questioned about their family? Paul states this expectation fairly strongly: "He must manage his own family well." However, he doesn't provide, here at least, evidences of a well-managed family.

Perhaps it is appropriate to highlight some of Paul's other teaching about family living. Passages in Ephesians 5–6 make good beginning places. Here he writes that a husband is to love his wife "as Christ loved the church and gave Himself up for her" (5:25), that "husbands ought to love their wives as their own bodies. He who loves his wife loves himself" (5:28), and that fathers should bring up their children "in the training and instruction of the Lord" (6:4).

Whatever other observations might be made, these passages and others argue strongly that one's wife and her development, interests, and needs ought to be among the husband's highest priorities. Even if it means giving yourself up, including your career and ministry, for the betterment of your relationship with your wife, that ought to be done. Certainly, we could argue that this is what it means at a minimum to manage "his own family well."

So too with the leader's children, for Paul states that they need to respectfully obey him (see also Ephesians 6:1). The implication seems to be that where there are disrespectful and/or disobedient children in the family, the father ought not "now" be considered for a leadership position.

It would seem at a minimum, therefore, that interviews of candidates for leadership positions should start with inquiries as to the qualities of character demonstrated and practiced by the candidate for a given position, particularly those positions which approximate that of "overseer." After this inquiry, the next level might well focus on the person's capacity to manage the family well. At the very least this should include an extensive interview with his wife and perhaps separate interviews with his children.

Paul's concern seems to be that the family is one of the most intensive management opportunities and experiences. It's tough to hide things from families. Children and their mother really know Dad. And if things are not "right and proper" in this essential relationship, there will be trouble in caring for church needs and responsibilities. As Paul states it: "If anyone does not know how to manage his own family, how can he take care of God's church?" (1 Timothy 3:5) Again, Paul seems to suggest that careful review of how one has managed his family gives valuable insight as to how one will manage the organization. By further implication, the leader ought not neglect his family after being given the leadership assignment. This must always be a priority in leadership.

Such teachings tend to be hard for us to handle, for several reasons. First, many tend to separate their family lives from their work lives. The thinking goes something like this: "It doesn't matter if there are unattended problems at home with my wayward children or if my wife and I are contemplating divorce. Indeed, that's nobody else's business as long as it doesn't interfere with the job." Second, others will argue that inquiries into family relationships are illegal. Yet here is an example where Paul clearly teaches that to hold a position of spiritual leadership, those kinds of inquiries are appropriate and necessary.

Proper management of one's family raises other questions. Does this include how I handle money and the other economic necessities of life? What about the extended family? Am I expected to manage the extended family as well or just myself, my wife, and my children? Is divorce evidence of an inability to manage the family well and therefore a disqualifier for spiritual leadership? At what age do children move outside parental responsibility and obedience? What about women in spiritual leadership roles? Am I to assume that since Paul only talks about men in these roles, women are not to be in them? If women are to be in these roles, do we simply transpose the word *wife*

41

for *husband* and vice versa? These are valid questions for further discussion.

9. *Not a lover of money, but pursuing honest gain* (verses 3, 8). Elsewhere Paul cautions us that the love of money is a root of all kinds of evil. So it is not surprising that he gives us this caution here. We know that contentment (see also Hebrews 13:5) with what God has provided ought to mark the way we live and further, that people who have the desire to get rich may ultimately end up in ruin and destruction:

> But godliness with contentment is great gain. For we brought nothing into the world, and we can take nothing out of it. But if we have food and clothing, we will be content with that. People who want to get rich fall into temptation and a trap and into many foolish and harmful desires that plunge men into ruin and destruction. For the love of money is a root of all kinds of evil. Some people, eager for money, have wandered from the faith and pierced themselves with many griefs (1 Timothy 6:6-10).

Peter also speaks words of caution to elder-shepherds about money:

> Be shepherds of God's flock that is under your care, serving as overseers—not because you must, but because you are willing, as God wants you to be; *not greedy for money*, but eager to serve; not lording it over those entrusted to you, but being examples to the flock. And when the Chief Shepherd appears, you will receive the crown of glory that will never fade away (1 Peter 5:2-4, emphasis mine).

Do these passages suggest that while it is not appropriate for overseers to love money or to be greedy for money, it *is* acceptable for non-overseer types of leaders to behave this way? Probably not. There are enough other passages in the Scriptures cautioning restraint in this area. Jesus' parable about the rich fool is one example (Luke 12:13-21). And the Lord continues in the same line of thought when He tells people not to worry about things that money can buy (verses 22-34).

These verses (and others) make a strong argument

that leaders and others ought not have the love of money as a reason for considering a leadership position. Paul also has as a separate yet related expectation that the means that are used to earn money should be honest and above-board. Nothing questionable is appropriate here. Otherwise one's reputation and respect by others may be called into question.

10. *Not a recent convert* (verse 6). It was Paul's observation that candidates for positions of spiritual leadership should not be recent converts. While he doesn't state any lapse of time that must take place, he does suggest that it should be long enough so that selection as a leader would not make the person conceited. Paul himself moved fairly quickly from being a person who persecuted Christ to one who became His loyal and faithful servant.

Often we are tempted to conclude that longtime Christians are those who are the most mature in the faith. My observations suggest that such is not necessarily the case. I have seen Christians who claim they have been growing Christians for thirty years when in fact they have repeated the same year of growth for thirty years. This group, perhaps, was the kind the writer of Hebrews had in mind in Hebrews 5:11-14 when he wrote about those still needing spiritual "pabulum" who should have been dining on more mature fare. I have seen other much younger Christians who have demonstrated incredible growth over only a very few years. So evidences of Christian growth, not just the passage of time, might be what Paul is getting at.

11. *Wives worthy of respect* (verse 11). In the same way that the husband-leader is to meet certain leadership expectations, so too should his wife (or presumably her husband?). Paul says it this way: "In the same way, their wives are to be women worthy of respect, not malicious talkers but temperate and trustworthy in everything." Presumably, if the husband is committed to and loves his wife as he ought, and manages his family well, this expectation would be a natural result of the process.

CONCLUSION

In this chapter we have attempted to look at and review some of the stated biblical expectations for leadership. We have made the following observations:

First, in many ways, the Scripture, rather than only discussing expectations for leaders, tends to clearly identify expectations for people who want to take their walk with Christ seriously. These expectations are found throughout the pages of Scripture and apply equally, in an organizational context, to both leaders and followers.

Second, there are some lists, on the other hand, which do speak to specific qualifications for spiritual leadership. Paul's list does not appear to be of the multiple-choice variety; that is, where the leader-candidate can pick several and ignore the rest. Rather, Paul seems to argue that the leader will exhibit *all* of these characteristics and that *all* are essential to leadership.

Third, there appear to be several marked differences with regard to leadership expectations for those who aspire to positions of spiritual leadership. For example, the spiritual leader ought to be preoccupied with internals of life rather than only externals. We know that God examines the heart and is vitally concerned about qualities of character. Leaders tend to be concerned about "how I look to man" when God is concerned about "how I look to Him." Further, many candidates for positions of leadership tend to focus on job-related characteristics when God looks primarily and initially at the heart-related ones. In addition, contemporary job searches tend to be heavy on references from business colleagues. The Scripture seems to suggest that one of the most telling references ought to be the candidate's wife or husband and the children.

I am not suggesting that prior experience in another church or other organization is unimportant. I am not suggesting that it is useless or unnecessary, through the processes of both education and experience, to gain and/or improve one's skills so as to enhance effective leadership. What I am suggesting and particularly with regard to spiritual leadership is that we ought never get to those other considerations if the heart is not right. Of what value are experience and degrees if the character is flawed? How will poor family relationships enhance leadership performance within an organization?

Once again the Scripture has identified fundamental essentials for spiritual leadership. Our job is to master them and to continue growing. It is a task for both leaders and followers.

QUESTIONS FOR FURTHER THOUGHT AND DISCUSSION

1. How would you address the questions I posed on page 34?
2. The context for Paul's lists in 1 Timothy 3 and Titus 1 is targeted for the church leader. How would you, or would you, apply these items to parachurch positions of leadership? What about to other positions of leadership within the local church such as choir director, usher, Sunday School teacher?
3. As honestly as you can answer this, have you ever been reviewed for a position of spiritual leadership according to either the list in 1 Timothy 3 or Titus 1? If so, was it done formally or informally? What was the reaction of your husband or wife to the process? What about that of the children?
4. In what ways does the list suggested by Paul seem practical or impractical? Does the list fit the 20th century? Why or why not?
5. In what ways is spiritual fitness for a given position related or connected to job fitness for that position? Isn't there a danger that overattention to spiritual fitness, at the expense of job fitness, will damage the effectiveness of the organization? What about the opposite position?
6. Assuming the absence of some committed sin such as adultery, embezzlement, and the like, do you know of "competent" leaders who have been dismissed from their positions of leadership for spiritual shortcomings? My hunch is that more people get dismissed because they didn't raise enough money, balance the budget, etc., than because they were spiritually deficient. Do you agree or disagree?
7. If Paul were once again sitting down to write another letter to Timothy on leadership, what items or teachings from 1 Timothy 3 (or Titus 1) would you advise him to delete or change? What items would you want him to add? Why?

CHAPTER
THREE

THE SPIRITUAL GIFTS
OF LEADERSHIP

We next want to look at just who is qualified to serve in a leadership role. Must the leader possess the spiritual gift of leadership? Does God distribute His gifts on the basis of sex or along some other line? *Is* leadership a spiritual gift? If so, does this mean that my formal educational preparation for leadership is irrelevant? And what about my experience in previous places of employment—is that too irrelevant to spiritual leadership? While we will not address all of these questions in this chapter, we do want to spend time on the difficult issue of spiritual giftedness as it relates to leadership.

CONFUSION ABOUT SPIRITUAL
GIFTEDNESS

The matter of discussing spiritual gifts (I have in mind passages such as Romans 12:6-8; 1 Corinthians 12:7-10, 28; Ephesians 4:7-8, 11-13; and 1 Peter 4:10-11) in ministry has not been without controversy. Persons far more knowledgeable than I have indicated their reluctance to deal with the matter. Tillapaugh's comment is illustrative:

> The topic of gifts is . . . too complex and controversial to be dealt with in the scope of this book. In fact, I recently heard a pastor I respect very much say that he would never try to help people discover their spiritual gifts. . . . A great deal of

confusion exists on the topic of spiritual gifts and I feel no compulsion to add to it.[1]

The respected writer on Christian leadership, Kenneth Gangel, adds a caution of his own as he writes on this subject: "No one is more aware than I that we venture at this point into a very controversial aspect of evangelical doctrine."[2]

The matter appears to be complicated and confusing for several reasons. I want to note only three here.

1. *People argue that those who don't have the spiritual gift of leadership ought not be leaders.* The assumption is that only a limited number of people have the spiritual gift of leadership. Therefore a key determination before a leader is appointed is whether or not such an aspirant is spiritually gifted to be a leader. As the argument goes, if one does not have the spiritual gift of leading, then one ought not be in a leadership position.

It is my opinion that some of the confusion on this point can be eliminated if we start with a different assumption, and further, distinguish between a leader and an officeholder. That assumption is: God bestows on every believer gifts that can influence others for the cause of the kingdom. One can be a leader and yet not hold an office or formal leadership role.

For example, I believe that all Christians to some extent have a bit of a leader in them. Note the words of John Stott, quoted by Gangel: "God has a leadership role of some degree and kind for each of us."[3] I share Stott's position on this point. There are few Christians anywhere who don't exercise some degree of influence in a godly direction over someone else to achieve some kind of God-honoring objective or to take some kind of God-honoring action, whether it be the church, home, or an organization. And as McKenna has noted: "*Every Christian* is called to be a follower of Christ and a leader of others" (emphasis added).[4]

However, it doesn't follow that everyone who exercises leadership in some informal way is necessarily interested in or qualified to hold a leadership office in the context of an organization. A person can be a leader within a given sphere of influence and yet can be totally disinterested in holding a formal position of leadership elsewhere.

As we have seen, the Scripture has some clear teaching as to the qualifications for the more formal officeholder. I find it to be of more than just passing interest that possessing the spiritual gift of leadership (Romans 12:8) is not one of the requirements stated by Paul in his lists setting forth qualifications for deacons and elders (1 Timothy 3:1-13; Titus 1:6-9). Do we not consider pastors or elders to be leaders? Do we err in our expectation that pastors *be* leaders? Perhaps the answer has something to do with our definitions of leadership and, further, our assumptions about just who leaders are.

As we observed, not everyone who "manages or administrates an office" is a leader. The occupant may be a superb administrator or manager but that alone may not make that person a leader.

2. *Confusion exists about how one receives or obtains the spiritual gift of "leadership."* For instance, does the Spirit of God make non-leaders into leaders? If so, is this progressive or a one-time, one-event occurrence? Is one born with the ability to lead or are leaders made? While I am not so presumptuous as to try to answer all of these questions, others have provided some useful commentary.

Clinton argues that in the context of leadership development, "the most important development during the middle sub-phase involves discovering spiritual gifts and using them confidently."[5] He then sets forth in sequence the eight phases of the "giftedness discovery process." He further defines spiritual gifts as "those special capacities given by the Holy Spirit to every believer and energized by the Holy Spirit in the believer's ministry."[6] He notes that "a spiritual gift is a unique capacity for channeling the Holy Spirit's power into a ministry."[7]

In his book *Ablaze for God*,[8] Duewel has a useful chapter (chapter 28) on this subject. His starting point appears to be the recognition that whatever ability we have must be viewed as God-given and is to be used for God's glory: "Every natural ability God gives us is a trust which we are responsible to use."[9] Duewel suggests that there are at least three types or groups of spiritual gifts listed in Scripture. First, he notes *the supernatural spiritual gifts*, or the gifts which are "completely dependent upon God's miracle power...." In this group are gifts having to do with matters such as prophecy, healings, the ability to speak in unknown languages, and the like. Leadership and administration do not appear to be included in this group.

The second group of gifts are those *"abilities with which we were born* or which we have developed."[10] These gifts Duewel refers to as *natural gifts.* All of us have seen in our children and in others the expression of these God-given natural gifts. Some people take a God-given gift and do nothing to develop or enhance it. Others take great lengths to do so. Whether or not the possessor of the gift recognizes the "natural gift" as a gift from a loving Heavenly Father, it is a God-given gift just the same. For the Christian, these kinds of gifts can be specially used of God: "God can add a special supernatural touch which supplements the natural gift with the divine, guides and empowers the natural skill with the supernatural supervision, and maximizes and multiplies the effectiveness by the enabling and anointing of the Spirit."[11]

The third group of spiritual gifts Duewel identifies are what he calls *practical gifts* such as "serving, administrating, encouraging, faith, giving, helps, knowledge...." My sense is that Duewel would include in this third group many of those practical vocational gifts that are listed in Old Testament references such as Exodus 35:30-35 and Exodus 36:1-2, 8.

Arthur Miller and colleagues writing in *The Truth about You,*[12] while certainly allowing for the expression of supernatural spiritual gifts, reflect Duewel's "natural gifts" approach to this matter of giftedness. At some risk of oversimplification, and relying on texts such as Psalm 139:13-14, their argument is that careful study of these and other verses will yield the conclusion that part of the process of shaping and knitting together in the womb includes God's giving to people individual patterns (biological, personality, interests, etc.) which influence future directions. These patterns are present at birth and will naturally work themselves out in the process of living life. As Miller observes: "People could ... only become ... who they were designed to be."[13] "People begin with a specific design that remains consistent through life and the design cannot be changed. This is not to say that there cannot be alterations in a person's life, since there are areas in people which need development or modification. . . . As astounding as this discovery was to us, there was no doubt as to the validity of this truth, after experiencing absolute consistency in case after case (more than three thousand cases). . . ."[14]

All of us have seen children demonstrate at an early age all kinds of different interests and abilities. Sometimes we see these same personality traits evident in either the mother or the father. Sometimes we see interests that are nowhere close to interests or aptitudes of the parents. The child who enjoys selling lemonade at age four not surprisingly is enjoying selling real estate, cars, bonds, ideas, at age thirty-five. The child who is preoccupied with numbers at age six not surprisingly ends up in a profession that requires considerable use of the manipulation of numbers and figures.

Each person, Miller argues, has been given groups of "motivated abilities" which can be developed through experience and enhanced through education. Miller argues that five key ingredients are in everyone's motivational pattern. First, the pattern has one primary motivational thrust. Second, "there is a recurring way of operating with others." Third, "there is a group of abilities present." Fourth, "there is recurring subject matter." Fifth, "there are recurring circumstances." One task of normal growth and development, then, is to ascertain, through study of my history, just what my motivational patterns are. With regard to vocational employment, then, my task is to find those positions which fit my pattern of God-given motivated abilities.[15]

Interestingly, these motivated ability patterns are given to people by the time of birth, which by implication means that both Christians and non-Christians receive them. These abilities can be further developed and enhanced by experiences and education. For the person who comes to know Christ personally, these abilities will be used to further His kingdom and to build up the body of Christ instead of being directed at the pursuit of only selfish interests.

Bruce Jones gives us a very solid discussion of this subject in his book *Ministerial Leadership in a Managerial World.* He sees that "spiritual gifts and natural talents are both a part of a biblical theology of management."[16] "Spiritual gifts, like natural talents, can be developed to varying degrees of effectiveness. And, finally, effectiveness for a Christian requires that our motive be for the glory of God and that our ministry be performed in the power of the Spirit."[17] Jones also provides a useful discussion of the offices of overseer, pastor, and elder[18] and offers additional insight on the "gift of leadership," quoting Peter Wagner as observing that "the gift of leadership for the minister is an essential prerequisite in church growth."[19]

I would recommend further study of these and other authors who have written on this important subject. Their efforts appear to be biblical, logical, and fit many observations we all have noted about Christian leaders and Christian leadership.

3. *Our own experiences have produced additional confusion about the spiritual gift of leadership.* All of us, for example, have observed Christians who have claimed the spiritual gift of leadership struggle in a formal leadership role. We have seen pastors who have acted as dictators "in the name of Jesus." We have seen people with "nice" personalities and a "happy" smile perform in dysfunctional ways in a formal leadership role. (I thank the Lord that there are many examples of positive leadership as well!)

We have also seen people with secular, non-Christian mindsets function well in leadership roles within the secular organization. Paradoxically, I have talked with many people who are part of Christian organizations who wish their organization were run in a way similar to some secular organization so that the employees would be treated with greater dignity and worth. All of us are aware of Christian organizational "nightmares" with regard to how personnel are cared for. Many Christian books dealing with leadership often cite with approval the work of some secular writers on this subject. And seeing the "successful" leadership of non-Christians raises questions about the nature of leadership as a "spiritual gift."

SORTING OUT SPIRITUAL GIFTS

Where does all this take us with regard to the spiritual gift of leadership? I understand that the Spirit doesn't operate by man's categorizations or lists and will do His work as He sees fit whenever and wherever He chooses. And so you, the reader, will need to study this further and draw your own conclusions. Nevertheless, here is how I approach this difficult subject. I make these comments with appropriate caution.

☐ *Natural gifts*

I start with the "natural gift" approach, noting that God, as an act of creation, shapes people in the womb according to certain intentional patterns and abilities. Each person is born as a gifted person, with gifts and abilities which can be redeemed for God's glory when the possessor commits himself or herself to Christ and becomes a Christ-one or Christian. But whether the person establishes a personal relationship to Christ or not, the element of giftedness (but not spiritual giftedness) still remains.

It follows, therefore, that whenever the possessor of these God-given abilities comes to accept Christ personally, these gifts are then given over to the Lord for His purposes, for His use and glory. Paul's teaching in Romans 12:1-2 is helpful to me here. This giving over to Christ of my body, which presumably includes God-given abilities, Paul calls an act of spiritual worship. The gifted musician who becomes a Christian gives to Christ the gifts and abilities of music as part of her spiritual worship. Many effective leaders of secular organizations who come to know Christ bring their leadership abilities to Christian organizations as part of their spiritual worship.

All of us have witnessed the good teacher who is empowered by the Holy Spirit as spiritual truths are being imparted. Further, as Christians, those exercising these types of gifts certainly must do so depending on the leadership of the Holy Spirit for strength. The work that is done is carried forth in the mighty name of Jesus.

☐ *Practical gifts*

"Practical gifts," such as administrating, encouraging, giving, and showing mercy, illustrate the fact that *all* Christians are gifted by God to meet a given need within the body of Christ.

52

As the person who names the name of Christ exercises these practical gifts empowered by the Holy Spirit, the gifts become spiritual gifts. Peter's words are instructive:

> Each one should use whatever gift he has received to serve others, faithfully administering God's grace in its various forms. If anyone speaks, he should do it as one speaking the very words of God. If anyone serves, he should do it with the strength God provides, so that in all things God may be praised through Jesus Christ. To Him be the glory and the power for ever and ever (1 Peter 4:10-11).

☐ *Supernatural spiritual gifts*
It appears that the Scripture teaches that certain spiritual gifts exist which are fully supernatural, wholly miraculous, though I would not include leadership among them. Of course I recognize and note that the Scripture also adds specific limitations on the use and purposes of these gifts. Further, however we define spiritual giftedness, we must observe that the purpose and results of spiritual gifts are for the benefit of the body of Christ, for the common good. Paul's words in Ephesians 4 explaining the "why" of giftedness are particularly helpful: "So that the body of Christ may be built up until we all reach unity in the faith and in the knowledge of the Son of God and become mature, attaining to the whole measure of the fullness of Christ" (verses 12-13).

☐ *The spiritual gift of leadership*
Is there the spiritual gift of leadership? Romans 12:6-8 clearly allows for that gift: "We have different gifts ... if it is leadership, let him govern diligently." But at the same time the text doesn't appear to clearly distinguish how one comes into possession of the gift of leadership. It could be a supernatural gift in the way that we have previously used the term. For example, I'm reminded of Saul, the future leader of Israel, as we see him in 1 Samuel 10:10: "The Spirit of God came upon him in power, and he joined in their prophesying." It might be a gift such as that given to Gideon, where it appears that a non-leader experienced God's blessing in an unusual way and became an effective leader. It might be the gift of leadership such as we see with Daniel, an effective leader throughout his lifetime.

Paul honed his intellectual and debating skills and then was captured by the Lord for a significant leadership role.

In brief, whether through supernatural endowment, whether God-given at birth, whether developed through broad and diverse experience, for the Christian, leadership at all levels, both informal and formal, needs to be viewed as a trust given by a loving Heavenly Father to be used for His purposes.

☐ *The formal "office" of leadership*

When we are considering people for positions of formal leadership, perhaps it's more helpful not to look solely at the source of the gift of leadership (because God is the source of all good gifts) but rather at *how* the gift might be or is being exercised, *toward what ends* would those efforts be directed, and perhaps most importantly, what is the *spiritual character* of the person being considered for leadership. As McKenna notes: "We learn that Christian leaders are different in 'being' as well as 'doing.' Our Incarnational 'being' is to embody the Spirit of Christ; our Incarnational 'doing' is to empower His people."[20]

Addressing these kinds of questions is particularly important for one being considered for a leadership role. Given the ends aspired to in leadership as well as the purposes for leadership, my hope would be that all who name the name of Christ would aspire to be a follower of Christ, to be indwelt and empowered by His Spirit, and to be a leader and a follower of others. As we pursue the work of the kingdom, "every Christian is called to be a follower of Christ and a leader of others."

QUESTIONS FOR FURTHER THOUGHT AND DISCUSSION

1. In the Christian organization, must the leader possess the spiritual gift of leadership? Is leadership a spiritual gift?
2. Does God distribute leadership gifts on the basis of sex?
3. Is formal education and experience relevant to the spiritual gift of leadership? How so? Why not?
4. Both Stott and McKenna suggest that every Christian is called to exercise leadership of some kind. Do you agree with this?

How would this impact my assertion that leaders follow and that followers lead?

5. Does the Spirit of God make non-leaders into leaders? If so, when and under what conditions?

6. Are leaders born or made? Please explain your answer.

7. What is your reaction to the Miller material? Do you see any patterns over your own life? What are some of them?

PERSONAL COMMITMENT IN LEADERSHIP

There is legitimate concern on the part of many in society that *commitment* is a word for an older and past generation. Commitment suggests a lack of freedom to make current choices. And if there is one value which governs contemporary society, it is the value that I can't jeopardize my ongoing freedom to make choices. As a result, we have adopted a contractual way of living which has infected much of what we do.

Classic "contract law" suggests, for example, that for a contract to be valid, the parties must each benefit and must each suffer a detriment or cost. For example, in the commercial world, if I want to purchase a car, I sign a contract which has benefits for both me and the car dealer. My benefit is that I now have a new vehicle. The detriment or cost to me is that I part with hard-earned cash. On the part of the dealer, the benefit is that she now has more money. The detriment or cost is that she now has one less car to own or control.

As was noted earlier, this concept from the commercial world has, in many ways, been carried over to the noneconomic areas of life. In terms of marriage, for example, the vows "until death do us part" have become subordinate to this contract view of commitment. "Vows" tend to be interpreted primarily as benefit from the marriage contract. When I cease to get the benefits I think I'm entitled to, I set about to break or otherwise modify the contract. "What's in it for me" tends to become the value of significance.

Robert Bellah and his coauthors of the secular best-seller *Habits of the Heart* make these observations about the ascendancy of this contract view over against that of the perceived value of commitment:

> The question "Is this right or wrong?" becomes "Is this going to work for me now?" By its own logic, a *purely contractual ethic leaves every commitment unstable.* Parties to a contract remain free to choose, and thus free to remake or break every commitment, if only they are willing to pay the price for doing so.... Perhaps a contract model ... cannot carry the weight of sustained and enduring commitments (emphasis mine).[1]

It can easily be seen that this contract mentality has multifold ramifications in many areas of life, whether job-related, the view of the family and family responsibilities, my view of the role of government and the citizen's responsibility, my view of whether or not I "owe" society or "am owed" by society, or indeed with regard to my relationship to God.

In many cases, this contractual view of life has defined the idea of commitment and, to the great regret of many, this secular version of commitment has permeated the church. First, the church itself has tended to insist on a revision of the New Testament idea of being a member and integral part of the body of Christ. The church has instituted, and equated in many cases, the idea of "membership" in the local organized church with being part of the body of Christ. Indeed, membership requirements or commitments bear some reflection to the idea of the contract we have previously discussed. Just as with a club membership, church members contract to attend faithfully, give funds, and adhere to group expectations and guidelines. In some circles, the church membership's policies and procedures acquire a spiritual quality and seemingly take the place of actual scriptural guidelines.

A second carryover effect of this contractual view of commitment comes with the perception of many in the local congregation that I have to adhere to my side of the membership agreement only as long as the local organized church lives up to its side. Obviously, as long as I am only a church "attender" and not a church "member," my commitments to the local organized church can remain rather minimal. Many times this also has a residual carryover effect in terms of my relationship to God—I only have to love and obey Him (i.e., remain committed) as long as He meets my needs, blesses me, and keeps me wealthy and healthy. In other words, He has a responsibility to live up to His end of the bargain, and I have a responsibility to live up to mine. As we will see elsewhere, it is questionable as to whether such a view of commitment is supported in Scripture.

A third way this view of life and its responsibilities can affect my mindset is that commitment is something that nobody has enough of and something everyone needs more of. In the context of the church, for example, I have heard literally dozens of sermons lamenting the lack of commitment on the part of church members. As a result, frequent appeals are made for persons in attendance to make a deeper commitment to Christ—to move *from* a position of being uncommitted or marginally committed to Christ *to* a position of total commitment to Christ. Obviously these appeals are in the right direction.

All of these comments are preliminary to the subject of this chapter—the leader as a committed person. Are people basically uncommitted? What do we mean by commitment? What is meant by total commitment? What are evidences of commitment? It's to the delineation of these and related matters that we now turn.

ALL LEADERS ARE COMMITTED TO SOMETHING OR SOMEONE

As I see the matter, the issue is not whether I am a committed person. Rather, the matter appears to be better stated this way: To whom and/or to what am I committed? All leaders are committed persons. Interestingly, this seems to be an *a priori* assumption of the Scripture as well. Seldom does the Scripture discuss committed or uncommitted people. It assumes, it seems to me, that people will be committed. With that assumption, it then presents options for commitment along with a corresponding appeal for commitments which are God-honoring. Several examples might be useful.

In Paul's letter to the Romans, he notes the tension between being dead to sin and being alive in Christ. He makes several observations, but one of particular note for our purposes is found in 6:16 where he asks his readers, almost rhetorically, the following question:

> Don't you know that when you offer yourselves to someone to obey him as slaves, you are the slaves to the one whom you obey—whether you are slaves to sin, which leads to death, or to obedience, which leads to righteousness?

Among other things, Paul seems to be saying that the issue isn't really one of whether or not one is committed or obedient. Rather, the issue remains *the object* of that obedience or commitment. And Paul presents us with only two choices at this point. We can choose to be slaves to sin, which leads to death, or we can choose to be obedient slaves to the teachings of Christ. It's almost as if he's saying, "That's it. These are your only choices when it comes to commitment. You can choose either sin or Christ. There's no middle ground." By extension, then, Paul does not allow for the seemingly middle ground of uncommitment. Rather, he encourages commitment to one choice or the other. Obviously, he argues that the right choice ought to be commitment to Christ.

This "no middle ground" position is also reflected in the Book of the Revelation, where Jesus voices this complaint against the church in Laodicea: "I know your deeds, that you are neither cold nor hot. I wish you were either one or the other! So, because you are lukewarm—neither hot nor cold—I am about to spit you out of My mouth" (3:15-16). We really ought not be surprised by this strong desire for commitment one way or the other because the Scripture consistently presents God as a jealous God (Exodus 20:5; Deuteronomy 4:24; Joshua 24:19).

Turning to one of many Old Testament examples, Joshua deals decisively with this matter of commitment. As a follower of Moses and ultimately his successor, Joshua successfully led the Children of Israel into the Promised Land. After Israel had "rest from all their enemies around them," Joshua called a meeting of all Israel—"their elders, leaders, judges, and officials"—and gave them a farewell address. The text of that beautiful challenge appears in Joshua 23–24. Significantly, one of the questions he put to the people was not whether or not they would be committed people, but rather to whom would they be committed.

> Now fear the Lord and serve Him with all faithfulness. Throw away the gods your forefathers worshiped beyond the River and in Egypt, and serve the Lord. But if serving the Lord seems undesirable to you, then choose for yourselves this day whom you will serve, whether the gods your forefathers served beyond the River, or the gods of the Amorites, in whose land you are living. But as for me and my household, we will serve the Lord (Joshua 24:14-15).

Again, two choices are presented. One can choose commitment to God, or one can choose to be committed to not serving God. We turn back to the New Testament for our third example.

In his second epistle Peter writes among other reasons to warn the people about false prophets and teachers. This is particularly the focus in chapter 2. After a variety of observations about false teachers, he makes this observation about mankind in general in verse 19: "For a man is a slave to whatever has mastered him." Whereas in the other passages two choices and related consequences are presented, Peter seems to be suggesting a further but similar point of departure: You can observe the object of commitment by viewing who or what has mastered (or controls) a person. Again, the issue is not whether or not one is living as a committed person. Rather, the concern seems to be to whom or to what am I committed. And, notes Peter, one can make that determination by observing the object or person of mastery.

The story is told of a man walking along one of the streets of Chicago wearing a sandwich board. As one approached this walking "advertisement" one would read these words: "I'm a fool for Christ." Obviously this brought chuckles and laughs of derision from onlookers. And then the viewer would read the back side of the sign as the man passed by: "Whose fool are you?" Stunned silence. That's the point of these verses on commitment. All of us, as committed persons, are somebody's fool. Whose fool are we?

WHAT ARE THE COSTS
OF COMMITMENT TO CHRIST?

Having a clear answer to the issue of commitment (yes, I am committed!) does not alone resolve the issue, for I must go yet a step further. Assuming I choose to be committed to Christ, what does that involve? As I view the matter, commitment to Christ is an act of the will which is based on my knowledge of Christ and my understanding of the costs involved. While, to be sure, there are costs associated with a choice not to be committed to serving Christ, our Lord made it very clear that there likewise are costs to being committed to serving Him. Let's look at several.

In Luke 9:23-27, Jesus makes sure His disciples are aware that this work of serving Him is potentially life-threatening. Perhaps the *Amplified New Testament* says it best:

> And He said to all, "If any person *wills* to come after Me, let him deny himself—that is, disown himself, forget, lose sight of himself and his own interests, refuse and give up himself—and take up his cross daily, and follow Me [that is, cleave steadfastly to Me, conform wholly to My example, in living and if need be in dying also]. For whoever would preserve his life and save it, will lose and destroy it; but whoever loses his life for My sake, he will preserve and save it [from the penalty of eternal death]" (verses 23-24, emphasis mine).

In verses 57-62 of that same chapter, Jesus again makes it clear that serving Him is a matter of greater urgency than having a regular place to sleep, of greater import than making funeral arrangements, and of more pressing concern than family good-byes. Jesus then wraps up His teaching by noting that the one committed to service in the kingdom doesn't look back to the former things: "No one who puts his hand to the plow and looks back [to the things behind] is fit for the kingdom of God" (verse 62, AMP). Jesus' point is obviously clear—there is a cost to serving Him. Commitment is costly!

Another Luke passage which deals with the subject of the cost of commitment is 14:25-33. In these verses, Jesus is explaining to the large crowds traveling with Him the costs associated with being committed to Him as a disciple. He notes that no one begins a construction project without first having funds to complete it. He observes further that one doesn't go to war without some assessment of the strength of the opposing army. Jesus then observes: "In the same way, any of you who does not give up everything he has cannot be My disciple" (verse 33). This appears to be yet another way of our Lord reminding us that we must count the cost of our commitment to serve Him.

CHRIST DESIRES AND DESERVES TOTAL COMMITMENT

This matter of Christian commitment is no part-time, easy task for the faint of heart. Christ desires all that I have and am. He instructs me as follows in Mark 12:30-31:

> Love the Lord your God with *all your heart* and with *all your soul* and with *all your mind* and with *all your strength*. The second [great commandment] is this: "Love your neighbor as yourself." There is no commandment greater than these (emphasis mine).

This expectation suggests total commitment. I ought not have much left over for me if I'm successful at loving Him.

Not only am I given a quantitative standard for loving Him, He also gives me a quantitative standard as to where this love for Him ought to fall in terms of my priorities. Note the following in Matthew 6:33:

> But seek *first* His kingdom and His righteousness, and all these things will be given to you as well (emphasis mine).

Obviously, pursuit of these types of quantitative standards will also yield qualitative results. More on that later. But we must go further.

To briefly review, Christ tells me how much I am to love Him and also which of my many conflicting priorities ought to be first. He then moves to specific expectations He has for my physical body:

> Do not offer the parts of your body to sin, as instruments of wickedness, but rather offer yourselves to God, as those

who have been brought from death to life; and *offer the parts of your body to Him* as instruments of righteousness (Romans 6:13, emphasis mine).

Therefore, I urge you, brothers, in view of God's mercy, to *offer your bodies as living sacrifices*, holy and pleasing to God—which is your spiritual worship (Romans 12:1, emphasis mine).

In addition to what we have already discussed in terms of commitment, there is still more. For not only must I seek first His kingdom, I must seek Christ first, for He is supreme. Note Colossians 1:18:

And He is the head of the body, the church; He is the beginning and the firstborn from among the dead, so that *in everything He might have the supremacy* (emphasis mine).

This kind of commitment, a commitment which acknowledges Christ, not me or another, as supreme, differs dramatically from the type of contractual commitment we discussed at the beginning of this chapter. In "therapeutic contracts" the focus for commitment is always on the self—what's in this for me? Will this help me or otherwise make me look good? Am I getting what I want? Obviously, the kind of commitment Christ demands of me goes substantially in another direction. As a result, that kind of commitment ought to make a major difference in the way I lead and follow.

WAYS TO EVALUATE MY COMMITMENT TO CHRIST

It's one thing to talk about my commitment to Christ. It's quite another to test or have that commitment tested. How can I do a commitment "checkup" as I honestly attempt with His help to serve as a leader? Let me suggest some evidences of intensive commitment to Christ.

1. *I will live contrary to the ways of the world.* Let me approach this from two different vantage points. I want to begin with Romans 12:2:

Do not conform any longer to the pattern of this world, but be transformed by the renewing of your mind. Then you will be able to test and approve what God's will is—His good, pleasing and perfect will.

The idea here of not conforming to the world's pattern has a similar focus in 1 John 2:15-16:

Do not love the world or anything in the world. If anyone loves the world, the love of the Father is not in him. For everything in the world—the cravings of sinful man, the lust of his eyes and the boasting of what he has and does— comes not from the Father but from the world.

Taking these verses together, we can make several observations. First, the passage in 1 John operationally defines the kind of world pattern identified in the Romans passage. Cravings, lusts, and boastings about possessions should find no room in the inn of Christian commitment. John flat out says that such matters come from the world. In the Romans passage, we are admonished to avoid conforming to that kind of world pattern. Clearly, Christ has something different for the committed Christian.

Second, the kind of nonconformity suggested by the Romans passage is an *internal* distinction, not an *external* one. Paul says it happens by the renewing of the mind. To be sure, there are external manifestations to what goes on internally within the mind. Earl Radmacher makes that point quite well in his book *You and Your Thoughts*.[2] Alternatively, in a Christian culture which is sometimes driven more by a focus on externals than a preoccupation with internals, Paul's enjoinder is a good one. We are transformed not by what we wear or don't wear; not by what kind of car we drive or don't drive; and certainly not by the kind of house we live or don't live in. Rather, we are transformed, through the power of the Holy Spirit, by the renewal of our minds.

Some in Paul's day, and obviously in our own, suggest that in order to avoid the pattern of the world, we must avoid the world and worldly people. Accordingly, we end up creating our own version of a nonworldly culture. Note Paul's response to this concern in 1 Corinthians 5:9-11:

> I have written you in my letter not to associate with sexually immoral people—not at all meaning the people of this world who are immoral, or the greedy and swindlers, or idolaters. In that case you would have to leave this world. But now I am writing you that you must not associate with anyone who calls himself a brother but is sexually immoral or greedy, an idolater or a slanderer, a drunkard or a swindler. With such a man do not even eat.

On to a third observation. Apart from the mind transforming process referenced in Romans 12:1, we will have difficulty knowing just what is God's "good, pleasing, and perfect will." Paul seems to be suggesting that my prayer for knowing God's will will not take place apart from experiencing a Spirit-indwelt, transformed, and renewed mind which is not conformed to the pattern of the world.

While more could be stated on this subject, it should be sufficient to observe that as one committed to Christ, and as a leader, I should be relentless in my pursuit of a transformed and renewed mind which is contrary to and not conformed to the patterns of the world.

2. *I will be prepared to experience and/or suffer persecution.* Jesus said it this way: "Remember the words I spoke to you: 'No servant is greater than his master.' If they persecuted Me, they will persecute you also. If they obeyed My teaching, they will obey yours also" (John 15:20). Paul made this observation: "In fact, everyone who wants to live a godly life in Christ Jesus will be persecuted" (2 Timothy 3:12).

Persecution doesn't appear to be a popular subject, at least among American Christians. Yet it appears to be an evidence of Christian commitment. Elsewhere around the world, committed Christians suffer daily for their faith in Christ. The paradox here is that we sometimes attempt to avoid the very persecution which for many believers serves to make their Christian faith strong and vital. Perhaps we ought to pray for more persecution. At the very least we ought to be involved in intercessory prayer for the strength and perseverance of Christian brothers and sisters around the world who daily do experience persecution.

3. *I will place little value on material things.* Jesus was not opposed to talking about money. Indeed, He talked

about money more than any other topic. Note this observation by Ron Blue in his book *Master Your Money:*

> Sixteen out of 38 of Christ's parables deal with money; more is said in the New Testament about money than heaven and hell combined; five times more is said about money than prayer; and while there are 500 plus verses on both prayer and faith, there are over 2,000 verses dealing with money and possessions.[3]

Yet as much as He discussed money or material things, Jesus never saw them as important, but as matters of little consequence and certainly as no cause for worry. For example, Jesus told His disciples not to worry about food, clothing, or the body: "And do not set your heart on what you will eat or drink; do not worry about it" (Luke 12:29). And He concluded His instruction by making this radical observation: "Sell your possessions and give to the poor. Provide purses for yourselves that will not wear out, a treasure in heaven that will not be exhausted, where no thief comes near and no moth destroys. For where your treasure is, there your heart will be also" (verses 33-34).

While Christ did not say material things were unnecessary, He clearly did not see such as being objects of great value. People who are committed to Christ will share this perspective about material possessions. On one's list of priorities, they will be near the bottom.

4. *I will gladly and willingly surrender my personal rights.* In a day and in a society which place a high premium on personal rights, this is a tough one. Some are quick to note, for example, that even Paul was not hesitant to invoke his rights of Roman citizenship. Nevertheless, and however difficult, personal rights for the Christian leader cannot hold center stage in the theater of life. Note Jesus' inclusive words in Luke 9:23-24:

> If anyone would come after Me, he must deny himself and take up his cross daily and follow Me. For whoever wants to save his life will lose it, but whoever loses his life for Me will save it.

While views vary as to what taking up one's cross means, it does seem from the context to mean that one needs to be willing to lose one's life. This seems to me to represent the ultimate denial of one's personal rights.

Once again, Christ is our example. When He was on the Mount of Olives on the way to the cross, He asked His Father to "take this cup from Me." Yet His prayer continued with these words: "Yet not My will, but Yours be done" (Luke 22:42).

Paul elaborates on this theme still further, particularly in Philippians 2:1-11, where he asks believers to model Christ's humility—a humility that caused Him to lay down His equality with God and become a man. If we claim commitment to Christ, we too must reflect this important evidence of our commitment in our leadership.

5. *I will be involved in the lives of others.* Significant involvement in the lives of others is a tough thing for many, particularly for "busy" leaders. Yet Jesus clearly envisioned that such would be the rule, not the exception.

For starters, He observed that the world's evidence that people were His disciples would be the love Christians have one for another. He said it this way in John 13:34-35: "A new commandment I give you: Love one another. As I have loved you, so you must love one another. All men will know that you are My disciples if you love one another."

These verses presume at least two things. First, loving someone else is essential. I can't love someone else if I don't share myself with others. This sharing myself with others is perhaps one of the things that Paul had in mind in Galatians 6:2 where he told us we are to bear one another's burdens and so fulfill the law of Christ. Bearing someone else's burdens or, conversely, having someone else bear my burdens, presumes a significant degree of involvement with others. Simply put, I must be and I will be involved with others.

Second, this loving relationship must in some way be visible to the world. My sense here is that while our focus must not be on loving for the sake of visible public relations, nevertheless, because truly loving one another reflects such a dramatic departure from the worldly pattern, the world *will* notice. In this same way, then, this is one reason why we ought to have a primary focus on unity within the body of Christ. Church splits, fights, quarreling, and the like, let alone visible and widely publicized expressions of human failure within the body of Christ, clearly do not draw "all men" to the conclusion that we are Christ's disciples.

I want to make yet a third observation at this point. As was the case with Paul in Romans 12:1-2, where the evidence of being not conformed to the world was the internal renewing of the mind, so too is the case here with our Lord's teaching. The evidence to the world, Jesus noted, will not consist of attention only to tangibles. Rather, the world will be drawn to our nontangible expression of love—love for one another—the kind of obedient love that sent Christ to the cross, the kind of tough love that Paul writes about in 1 Corinthians 13. To be sure, the expression of this kind of love might properly involve tangibles. But the primary expression ought to be on the love which results and produces a tangible expression of love and not the other way around.

6. *I will not be ashamed of Christ and His words.* I want to note Christ's seemingly clear teaching on this matter in Mark 8:38 (AMP):

> For whoever is ashamed [here and now] of Me and My words in this (unfaithful) adulterous and (preeminently) sinful generation, of him will the Son of Man also be ashamed, when He comes in the glory (splendor and majesty) of His Father with the holy angels.

Unfortunately, many churches have limited their application of this verse to the "altar call." Persons in attendance "at church" hear the pastoral reminder that if they are unwilling to get up in front of their Christian friends attending church with them, they violate this verse, which the pastor then quotes. While indeed this may not be a misapplication of the verse, it seems that our Lord is more concerned that His name and words be upheld, by people who are committed to Him, in front of people who are sinful and adulterous. This does not sound very much like the congregation in the local church. On the other hand, maybe it does. Inasmuch as Christ's teaching on this point also appears in the same Luke passage that discusses the need for one to "deny himself," the maintenance of this kind of unashamed testimony of one's love for Christ in front of a watching pagan world is evidence of commitment to Christ.

THE PROCESS OF COMMITMENT IS ONGOING

I want to make it clear that I'm not dealing here with one's salvation experience. Rather, what I have in mind is the path one takes following the conversion experience.

God's instructions to Joshua after the death of Moses included the following: "Do not let this Book of the Law depart from your mouth; meditate on it day and night, so that you may be careful to do everything written in it. Then you will be prosperous and successful" (Joshua 1:8). The sense of this verse is not that Joshua was to follow God's instruction only one time. Rather, the activity was to be continuous.

Jesus' disciple Peter instructs us, "But grow in the grace and knowledge of our Lord and Saviour Jesus Christ" (2 Peter 3:18). He also tells us that we are to "grow up in [our] salvation" (1 Peter 2:2). The process, as I see it, is the ongoing process of giving as much of myself as I know to as much of Christ as I know. In other words, as I get to know myself better and better, and as I grow in my understanding of Christ, and learn more about what He desires for my life, I am constantly bringing to Him new areas of my life for Him to control.

One illustration that Paul gives us of this process is found in Philippians 3:12-14:

> Not that I have already obtained all this, or have already been made perfect, but I press on to take hold of that for which Christ Jesus took hold of me. Brothers, I do not consider myself yet to have taken hold of it. But one thing I do: Forgetting what is behind and straining toward what is ahead, I press on toward the goal to win the prize for which God has called me heavenward in Christ Jesus.

One idea here is that while I may appreciate what God has done in the past, I can't continue to live there. As did Paul, we too must press on and grow in our commitment to Christ.

CONCLUSION

We began this chapter with some observations about society's eroding view of commitment, and how it in many ways has become relative and contractual in nature, based greatly on the benefit to the individual. We.then moved to a discussion for our need to be totally committed to Christ and the need for that commitment to be dynamic and growing.

We end our discussion of commitment with the reminder that our relationship with our Heavenly Father is *not* contractual in nature. Rather, the relationship we have is based on what He has done for us, not on what we do for Him. Author Walter Wangerin Jr., in his book *As For Me and My House,* reminds us of this very powerful, "fly in the face of society" truth:

> He manifested mercy, a perfect love; he canceled the old covenant with another one, altogether different, altogether new, in which the obligations were altogether one-sided, altogether his. He chose to love people unworthy of his love; he chose to be the God of the undeserving. "While we were helpless," says Paul, "at the right time Christ died for the ungodly.... God shows his love for us in that while we were yet sinners Christ died for us." The new covenant was offered in the blood of Jesus Christ.
>
> No longer is there a giving for a getting; we give absolutely nothing to get this love. No longer is it an exchange, faithfulness for faithfulness; God was faithful to the faithless, to sinners. No longer is the act of God reasonable or even legal; rather it is the abandonment of law itself. It is gratuitous, a perfectly free giving on his part, to save the "weak," "ungodly" transgressors of the covenant: instead of holding them to terms, he dismissed the terms from them.
>
> This new relationship is one in which something indeed comes from nothing, since we the people neither deserved nor could earn what we received from God.[4]

All of us need to pursue more intently this loving God of great commitment to us, the One whom we love because He first loved us (1 John 4:19). This same model of intense commitment is particularly the need for us who lead and for us who follow.

QUESTIONS FOR FURTHER THOUGHT AND DISCUSSION

1. Knowing there are different levels of commitment to Christ (a review of the following references, for example, illustrate Peter's progression of commitment: John 1:42; Matthew 4:18-20; 19:27; John 6:68-69; Luke 22:54-62; Acts 4:19-20; 5:41; 10:1-48), should this make a difference in hiring or other personnel decisions? Of what concern should this be to a board with regard to the selection of the CEO?

2. Given the context of 20th-century America, what have you forsaken to follow Christ? What or who ought you forsake which, by doing so, would enhance your commitment to Christ? What shifts in your priorities would assist you in this task? Does your job and/or other "outside" activities draw you toward or away from serving Christ more effectively?

3. If annually you were to give yourself a score on your "commitment checkup," and assuming you asked your family to evaluate you as well, would the scores of your children and/or spouse be anywhere near your own? What if you did the same thing for your colleagues at work? Your neighbors?

4. As a leader what are some of the ways you experience persecution for holding high the name of Christ?

5. Given Christ's emphasis on material possessions, are you satisfied that the kind of emphasis you place on them is about right? Too little? Too much? What percentage of your time is spent on the pursuit of material possessions? What changes must be made? When?

6. As a followup to question 5, in and of themselves, is possession of material things wrong? Why or why not? Is there a time when possession of things becomes wrong? When?

7. React candidly to the biblical idea of forfeiting personal rights. Does this mean one can never hire a lawyer or go to court? Express a grievance? Should I insist that terms and conditions of my employment be given to me in some kind of a written contract? What about union membership? What kind of personal rights should one not be giving up? Any? Would you insist on the same rights in other parts of the world, say on the foreign mission field in a Third World country? Why or why not?

8. How many really good, "let it all hang out" friends, other

than your spouse, do you have? Do you believe this is a problem? Should it be? In your opinion, about how many really good friends should you have? Is it possible to be significantly involved with others who are not really good friends? You're currently "bearing the burdens" of how many people?

9. In order to let the world see "good works" which will draw people to the Father, should "good works" be publicized?

10. Given our Lord's concern that we need to avoid being publicly ashamed of Him and His words, should you always bow your head at lunch when you know to do so will offend your superior and her lunch guests? If you're at a working business conference that goes through Sunday, do you skip "valuable" Sunday sessions in order to attend "church"?

CHAPTER
FIVE

LEADERSHIP AND OBEDIENCE

Simply put, *obedience* is one of the nasty words of the 20th century. It is perhaps less nasty to the leader-types who believe that their role is to command people, to issue orders, not to obey them. Such persons take great comfort in verses such as Hebrews 13:17: "Obey your leaders and submit to their authority. They keep watch over you as men who must give an account. Obey them so that their work will be a joy, not a burden for that would be no advantage to you."

To follower-types, however, the word has a perjorative ring to it. To them, obedience suggests images of the severe taskmaster and his subjects cowering before him. When the adjective *blind* is added as a qualifier to obedience, the negative images become even more heightened.

Obedience suggests an order giver and an order obeyer. It suggests a higher authority. And in our enlightened age where we are driven by such concepts as participative government and management, we don't take kindly to orders, only suggestions and guidelines. To obey, therefore, is hard enough. To obey blindly brings forth all of our remaining cultural resentments and resistance.

The dictionary defines *obedience* along these same lines: "act or practice of obeying; dutiful or submissive compliance; a sphere of authority, or a body of persons, etc., subject to some particular authority, especially ecclesiastical." In a society that strives for an egalitarian approach to many things (except in athletics!), obedience is not an easy concept to discuss, let alone practice. The typical Sunday School discussion comment that "wives are to obey their husbands" does little to ease our uncertainties or anxieties.

When I think about the concept of obedience, a couple of Scriptures come to mind immediately. One is the verse from Hebrews mentioned earlier in this chapter. The other is: "Children, obey your parents in the Lord, for this is right" (Ephesians 6:1). The latter verse stands out more prominently in my mind because of its seeming frequent use during my childhood days. What verses about obedience come to your mind?

If we're honest, we leaders tend to practice the idea of selective obedience. For instance, when we think it is in our best interest to have another practice obedience, then we think obedience is a great concept. For example, parents believe it is positive for their children to obey them. Business people expect that the terms of a contract, whether for the sale/purchase of a home or car, or a rental agreement, will be adhered to. Judges can reasonably expect that the terms of a court order will be obeyed. Physicians expect patients to obey their medical instructions. The motorist is always expected to obey rules of the road, including speed limits. And the military commander can expect that orders will be followed and obeyed.

On balance, then, most of us would probably agree that to obey is a good thing for society. Indeed, it is difficult to see how a society would function properly without some commitment on the part of its citizenry to the practice of obedience. Yet to those who desire diligence in both their walk with Christ and in their leadership, obedience is still a difficult concept.

For the leader, the Scripture has much to say about obedience. While we may readily see the importance of obedience in the areas just listed, we somehow lose sight of the fact that as children of the Heavenly King, we are to reflect obedience in our lifestyle. We need to both think and practice obedient Christian living.

Jesus identifies this point very clearly in the Gospels, particularly as recorded in the Book of John where He says:

If you love Me, you will obey what I command (14:15).

Whoever has My commands and obeys them, he is the one who loves Me. He who loves Me will be loved by My Father, and I too will love him and show Myself to him (14:21).

You are My friends if you do what I command (15:14).

Among other things these verses suggest directly or by implication the following ideas:

- ☐ He measures my love for Him more by how I act than by what I say;
- ☐ Walking in obedience to His commands counts for more than does mere spiritualized rhetoric; and
- ☐ I am how I act, not what I believe.

It is on this latter point that we evangelicals struggle, because many times we have substituted our talk in place of an obedient walk. We have impressed ourselves so much with our theologically correct language that we have overlooked God's preoccupation with our obedience to His commands and instructions. I want to carefully note at this point that I am not arguing against precision in the use of theological language. What I am arguing for, rather, is that right talk which isn't likewise coupled to right action doesn't appear to count for much in our Lord's evaluation.

I'm reminded at this point of Paul's statement to the Corinthians in 1 Corinthians 13:1 about the spiritual emptiness ("resounding gong . . . clanging cymbal") of hollow action. The Book of James is an equally excellent example of the biblical concern that right and obedient action be the true measure of spirituality. A person should be able to live with me and observe my actions for a period of time and then tell me what I believe. No exceptions to this biblical principle for those in leadership positions. The leader must readily and willingly practice obedient Christian living as a way of life. Why? Because Christ is our model for obedience.

CHRIST LEARNED OBEDIENCE

It is important to note that Christ *learned* obedience. Let's look, for example, at Hebrews 5:7-9:

During the days of Jesus' life on earth, He offered up prayers and petitions with loud cries and tears to the One who could save Him from death, and He was heard because of His reverent submission. Although He was a son, *He learned obedience* from what He suffered, and, once made perfect, He became the source of eternal salvation for all who obey Him (emphasis mine).

The text indicates that Jesus Christ learned obedience as a son through suffering and was made perfect. As a result, He has become the source of eternal life "for all who obey Him." Most of us would prefer to be in charge and "demand obedience" to our expectations. It is harder still to learn and practice obedience to another's expectation or command. Yet learn we must if we are to faithfully follow and lead.

CHRIST PRACTICED OBEDIENCE

Not only did our Lord learn obedience, He *practiced* obedience. While a number of Scriptures come to mind which make this point, one of my favorites is Philippians 2:5-11, a passage we have previously considered. We must note that while this text was addressed to "all the saints" at Philippi, Paul makes special note that "all the saints" includes the deacons and overseers (Philippians 1:1). So he could have just as readily begun verse 5 this way: "Now listen up, all you saints, including you leader-type deacons and overseers. Your attitude should be the same as Christ's." Paul doesn't use "cop-out" words such as *similar* or *like* when describing Christ's attitude. Rather, he makes it clear that our attitudes should be the *same* as that of Jesus Christ. That's an exceedingly high standard. And in a "my rights"-driven society, that's an exceedingly tough standard. Yet it's the biblical standard.

Then Paul so movingly and beautifully tells us once again this story of Christ. Even though He was God, He did not see equality with God to be something He, Christ, should strive for. Rather, Christ humbled Himself and became *"obedient* unto death—even death on a cross" (verse 8, emphasis mine). What a powerful example and model for the leader who struggles with submission and obedience.

THE BIBLICAL CASE FOR OBEDIENCE

Both the Old and New Testaments make a compelling case that obedience to the commands of Scripture is an essential part of biblical living. Indeed, in some ways, one could argue that the Scriptures are preoccupied with the concept of obedience. Some have argued, rightly in my opinion, that the major decision for the Christian is whether or not to be faithfully obedient to the commands of the Scripture.

I emphasize this concern about obedience for several reasons. Many times in my own selective obedience pertaining to "nonspiritual" matters, I tend to carry over a similar attitude with regard to spiritual ones. Simply put, this makes me a terrible follower of the living Christ. Further, if I selectively follow only those commands of the Scripture that I want to, and declare all the rest to be optional or unnecessary, I will not be the leader He wants me to be. So disobedience adversely impacts both my ability to lead and my capacity to follow.

In the remainder of this chapter, I want to review selected passages as examples of this important biblical imperative, first from the Old Testament and then from the New.

☐ *Samuel and Saul* (1 Samuel 15:1-22)

In this passage the writer makes it painfully clear that religious exercises are not a substitute for obedience to a clear command of God. Even though Saul was right in wanting to have a sacrifice offered to the Lord before going into battle, he had previously been instructed that he was not the one to offer the sacrifice. Yet Saul went ahead and offered the sacrifice anyway—and it cost him the kingdom. The telling words are found in verses 22-23 (TLB):

> Samuel replied, "Has the Lord as much pleasure in your burnt offerings and sacrifices as in your obedience? Obedience is far better than sacrifice. He is much more interested in your listening to Him than in your offering the fat of rams to Him. . . . And now because you have rejected the word of Jehovah, He has rejected you from being king."

Saul's failure to obey the word of the Lord had a devastating impact on his ability to lead. Because he was not a good follower, it cost him the opportunity to lead.

☐ *Moses and the Children of Israel* (Deuteronomy 5:1, 29; 6:1-3; 8:1; 10:12-13; 11:1; 26:16-18; 28:1)

In these passages, Moses is reviewing for the Children of Israel the things they need to know about their relationship with God as they anticipate their new lives in the Promised Land. While the specific commands Moses sets forth are intended solely for the Israelites, we see very clearly God's preoccupation with the need for the people to be obedient to His commands.

☐ *God and Israel* (Isaiah 29:13-14; Amos 4:4; 5:21-23)

These passages are again directed to God's chosen people. In Isaiah God calls up short His people for claiming to belong to Him while continuing to practice disobedience. He specifically cites His concern for their worship and the fact that it amounts to "mere words learned by rote" (verse 13, TLB). The specific concern according to the Amos references is that the people apparently thought that if they followed certain religious practices (if, for example, they offered regular sacrifices to God, practiced consistent tithing, and had a first-rate music program), they would honor the Lord. But here, the Scripture makes it clear that the pursuit of these otherwise seemingly appropriate activities by themselves, when God wanted pure hearts coupled with obedience to other commands, was both inadequate and unacceptable.

☐ *The temptation of Jesus* (Matthew 4:1-4)

In this passage, Jesus, obviously hungry after just finishing a forty-day fast, is approached by Satan who offers a suggestion as to how He might get food (turning stones into bread). Jesus answers with a strong no and then reaffirms the critical role that obedience plays in providing "real" sustenance for living: "Bread won't feed men's souls: obedience to every word of God is what we need" (verse 4, TLB). Jesus makes it very clear that obedience to the Word of God is critically important to life itself. Indeed, it's more important than physical food.

☐ *The Beatitudes* (Matthew 5:3-20)

In this portion of the Sermon on the Mount Jesus makes clear that He wants more than just talk about the commands of Scripture. It is those who *obey* or practice these commands who are great in the kingdom of heaven. Our

Lord wants more than just outward displays of righteousness, which the Pharisees apparently were good at. Followers of Christ are to practice inward righteousness—something man can't see but which is highly visible to God.

☐ *Judging others* (Matthew 7:21-22)

Jesus again warns His listeners to beware of those religious types who talk about God but don't practice His commands. Again, note His words: "The decisive question is whether they *obey* My Father in heaven" (verse 21, TLB; emphasis mine).

These verses and dozens more elsewhere in Scripture make it clear to the leader that disobedience to the Scripture is never an option. Whether responding to the board or to the various other constituencies of an organization, the place to start is not "thus saith the people" or "thus saith the board" but "thus saith the Lord." And my sense of this "thus saith the Lord" perspective is that such can never run counter to the revealed "word of God." As a leader, once I submit myself to being obedient to the Father in heaven, it follows that I must be both a hearer and a doer of His Word.

OBEDIENCE IN ORGANIZATIONS

I make the "thus saith the Lord" qualification for several reasons. First, where people who name the name of Christ come together in a corporate arrangement to do work for pay under conditions and terms imposed by external authority or by the organization itself, everyone involved in the association has submitted themselves to a higher (spiritual) authority and implicitly has agreed to be a "direction taker." The ultimate source of direction as to how we deal with one another in organization, then, becomes the Scripture.

An operative expectation must be communicated at every level in a Christian organization, which goes something like this: "We try to run this organization based on biblical principles. When you see us doing something that appears to run counter to the clear teaching of Scripture, you have the responsibility and obligation to point that out to us so we can correct the error." How better to communicate to all in the organization the answer to the question of ultimate obedience. All of us are called to be obedient first of all to Him.

And this leads to a second reflection about a commitment to a "thus saith the Lord" perspective within the organization: Such a perspective will not be pursued in isolation of or to the exclusion of insights from other believers involved in the association. Too many times, leaders claim by practice that they alone have the "private line" to God and He leaves everyone else out in the cold. Indeed, to even raise questions about the leader's private revelation is taken by these types of leaders to show disrespect and insubordination.

My experience is quite to the contrary. Indeed, I have found that when some action is clearly of the Lord it will usually be confirmed in the hearts of others by the same Holy Spirit who confirms it in mine. Assuming the presence of spiritual maturity on the part of persons in the workforce, it would be frightening to take a radical course of action that didn't have the confirmation, support, or even acquiesence of other brothers and sisters within the organization.

Does that mean that no action is taken by the leader until everyone agrees with the choice recommended? Obviously not. What it does mean is that usually there will be general support, however that support level is ascertained, for an action taken or anticipated. Notice I didn't say "agreement with." Rarely does everyone agree with every action taken in the association. Are there times when the leader must decide to take action which doesn't have the support of others in the association? Probably, assuming the action anticipated is not counter to the clear teaching of Scripture. But I would see this happening only on the rarest of occasions. This approach forces all to listen for the "thus saith the Lord."

In brief, then, the biblical standard of obedience clearly communicates to all that for both the "order taker" and the "order giver," there is a higher standard that all must be alert to. And that standard is the reality and necessity for all who name the name of Christ, including leaders who follow and followers who lead. Both need to profess and practice obedience to the clear teachings of Scripture.

There are simply no options for the leader to be disobedient to this standard.

Further, adherence to this standard, when taken seriously, provides a kind of protection to all others involved in the association, regardless of rank or function. For when I as a leader publicly declare my allegiance to Christ and my willingness to be obedient to the teachings of Scripture, I am in essence saying that I will let the Scripture govern how I act toward others in the organization. By implication and for example, I give up my right to act arbitrarily and capriciously within the organization. But how do I come to know the standards which I must commit myself to? Stated another way, how can I be obedient to His commands which impact how I operate in the organization if I don't know what those commands are? Indeed, if ignorance is bliss, would I not be better off not knowing biblical commands so I don't have to obey them?

The answer, of course, depends on the extent to which I want to take my commitment to Christ seriously. It seems implausible that I would, on the one hand, talk about wanting to be a faithful and obedient follower of Christ and on the other, to argue that if I don't really know the kinds of biblical expectations the Scripture has for me as a leader, then I don't need to be obedient to them.

Thus far in this chapter we have identified the high priority that the Scriptures give to obedience in the daily walk with Christ. In the next section of this chapter, I want to look more carefully at some of the specific scriptural expectations which demand my obedience. The verses that I identify are illustrative only. There are many, many more. They are verses that have been meaningful to me, so their inclusion here gives you some idea of the things in an organization that I believe are important. Again, you will need to study in context the verses listed.

SELECTED BIBLICAL EXPECTATIONS
REQUIRING OBEDIENCE

James 4:17. "Anyone, then, who knows the good he ought to do and doesn't do it, sins."

This is one verse I really don't like. In the first instance, it defines sin as an omission rather than something

I commit. If I have been taught over the years that sin just means doing bad things—such as slander, murder, stealing, adultery, and other acts similar to those listed in places like Galatians 5:19-21—and if I don't commit any of those sins, then I am home free. Right? Wrong!

This verse clearly identifies as sin lost opportunities to do good to others. My mind is immediately drawn to Galatians 6:10 where the instruction is that as I have opportunity I am to do good to all people, especially to other believers. I am also reminded of Jesus' conversation with the rich young ruler and that this young leader-type had kept the Law. Yet when Jesus reminded him that he was to rid himself of his possessions to help the poor, he struggled, and ultimately was not able to be a follower of Christ. Stated another way, the rich young ruler had a good score on his sins-of-commission test. But on his sins-of-omission exam, he failed.

I don't like James 4:17 for a second reason. In the organization, leaders are not always on the lookout for opportunities to do good to others. Why? Perhaps for the same reason the rich young ruler had such a difficult time with the command of Jesus—it costs money. Oh, maybe we provide flowers for an illness or death; perhaps we give a party at retirement time. Perhaps we send a pre-signed card for birthdays. Some argue that the good we do comes in the form of a paycheck and liberal fringe benefits. We may attempt to justify our doing good other ways. But, by and large, there is much room for improvement here. And improve I must if I am to be obedient to Scripture.

Mark 12:30-31. "Love the Lord your God with all your heart and with all your soul and with all your mind and with all your strength. The second [command] is this: 'Love your neighbor as yourself.' There is no commandment greater than these."

This too is a difficult command for me to obey. Without belaboring the point of just what exactly is meant by "heart, soul, strength, and mind," the meaning of the verse at least suggests that what Christ expects of me is love for Him which is total and complete. And if that is not tough enough, then He throws in the teaching about loving our neighbor as ourselves. And He gives us the Parable of the

Good Samaritan elsewhere (Luke 10:25-37) to answer the "And who is my neighbor?" question.

Whether defining neighbor in a geographical sense (the one next door, down the street, etc.) or more broadly as Jesus did in the Parable of the Good Samaritan, many leaders struggle with relating to neighbors. Perhaps it's due to the long hours required on the job or the long distances traveled. In the organizational context, loving my neighbor may not be any easier, because he may be my business competitor. But again, love my neighbor I must if I am to be obedient to Scripture.

Perhaps this was one of the reasons Jesus' prayer in John 17 focused on the need for unity among Christians. Perhaps He knew that unity among the brethren would be tough and therefore unity displayed to the world would be a very powerful evidence that Christ had been sent from the Father.

One of my great disappointments as I have viewed churches and other Christian organizations over the past two decades is the admitted lack of willingness to apply this "love your neighbor" teaching to "the competition." If you are a pastor, how closely do you work with nearby churches outside your own denomination? The same could be said about competitor Christian colleges and universities. I am persuaded that Christ's kingdom will be advanced more by our working together than by our working independently. I am tired of seeing denominational idolatry unashamedly exhibited across many denominations. My heart is grieved when I see greater interest and commitment given to denominational mandates and distinctives than I do to the clear teaching of Scripture.

Ironically, this "we don't need you to be our neighbor" attitude vanishes when mission field activities are encountered. On mission fields around the world there are countless examples of denominations working together as neighbors in ways that are unheard of in many parts of North America. Why? Because of need. Here is but another example of where Christ's concern for neighborliness has been celebrated in individuals but has been lost or abandoned in organizations.

Joshua 1:8. "Do not let this Book of the Law depart

from your mouth; meditate on it day and night, so that you may be careful to do everything written in it. Then you will be prosperous and successful."

Preoccupation! Preoccupation with the Scriptures! This appears to be a primary focus of this verse. Meditation presumes there is substance to be meditated on. This leads nicely into Scripture memory, one of the forgotten spiritual disciplines. As a leader-follower my thoughts must be preoccupied with the Scriptures.

Joshua 1:8 further suggests that I must be obedient to the commands contained in the Scripture: "Be careful to do everything written in it." The context of this command is that God was giving Joshua, the leader, his marching orders for leading the Children of Israel into the Promised Land. The verse also indicates, at least for Joshua, that if he would be faithful in this matter of obedience, he would be prosperous and successful.

I remain persuaded that I will be an effective leader only as long as I remain faithful to hearing, reading, studying, memorizing, and meditating on the Scriptures. Without this perspective, how will I know what I am to be obedient to? Only as my daily life and my personal and professional responsibilities are viewed through this scriptural grid do I have the opportunity to practice faithful, consistent Christian living.

Psalm 119:9, 11. "How can a young man keep his way pure? By living according to Your word. . . . I have hidden Your word in my heart that I might not sin against You."

One focus of these verses is purity of life, an exceedingly important priority for the leader. The psalmist reminds us that he has hidden the Scripture in his heart so that he can avoid sin in his life. The implication seems to be that if I am not doing the same, I am setting myself up to commit sin. The writer of the Book of James (James 1:13-15) makes it clear that sin many times results as impure thoughts become impure actions.

Elsewhere in the Psalms (Psalm 1) I am reminded that the righteous person, among other things, gives deliberate attention to meditating on the Scripture, something one cannot do apart from knowledge of the Scripture. So once again, I've come full circle with the obedience factor in leading and following, this time in the form of meditation and Scripture memory. I must do so to be an effective leader.

1 Thessalonians 5:16-18. "Be joyful always; pray continually; give thanks in all circumstances, for this is God's will for you in Christ Jesus."

These verses indicate the attitude that ought always characterize an effective leader. When a balanced budget looks like an impossibility, I am to remain joyful and be thankful. When I have a tough decision to make, I am to pray continually. This ought to be the way I approach my personal and professional life, regardless of the circumstance, decision, or individual involved. Then the writer indicates, for emphasis, that maintenance of this attitude is God's will for me.

I don't know about you, but this is difficult for me. I want to complain about problems. And the reality is that many times my complaint is justifiable, at least from a human perspective. But if I am to be an obedient follower of Christ, my options, as set forth here, are quite clear. Will I choose to be obedient, or won't I?

2 Timothy 2:24. "And the Lord's servant must not quarrel; instead, he must be kind to everyone, able to teach, not resentful."

Again, this verse contains excellent instructions for the leader. As I serve the Lord, I am given a clear mandate about what I can and cannot do in relationship with God's people. What better instructions could there be for a leader than to be kind to everyone? This suggests an evenness and a consistency of performance. I must be able to teach and be teachable, both indispensable elements to leading and following. Again, my task here is to be obedient to these instructions. Am I? Are you?

Hebrews 13:5. "Keep your lives free from the love of money, and be content with what you have, because God has said, 'Never will I leave you; never will I forsake you.'"

Many Christian leaders I have observed and talked to are not motivated by money, not to say that they are indifferent to it. But if anyone is on the borderline on this issue, this verse ought to get him off the fence—we are not to love money. I remember one fund-raising call with a secular business executive whose opening greeting to me was, "Boy, do I love money!" He then proceeded to tell me about all the things that money could buy, such as cars, vacation homes, and the like. The particular individual had obviously crossed the fence. Our attitude about money is to enjoy what money God provides, but to be content in our circumstances, particularly so when we think we need more and He doesn't.

Colossians 4:6. "Let your conversation be always full of grace, seasoned with salt, so that you may know how to answer everyone."

As a leader I ought to practice soft answers and avoid grievous words. I ought to reflect graciousness and respect for others in my speech. My conversations ought to be characterized by wisdom and tact. Again, tough commands, but ones I must be serious about if my desire is to obey Christ.

Luke 4:16-21. "He went to Nazareth, where He had been brought up, and on the Sabbath day He went into the synagogue, as was His custom. And He stood up to read. The scroll of the Prophet Isaiah was handed to Him. Unrolling it, He found the place where it is written: 'The Spirit of the Lord is on me, because He has anointed me to preach good news to the poor. He has sent me to proclaim freedom for the prisoners and recovery of sight for the blind, to release the oppressed, to proclaim the year of the Lord's favor.' Then He rolled up the scroll, gave it back to the attendant and sat down. The eyes of everyone in the synagogue were fastened on Him, and He said to them, 'Today this Scripture is fulfilled in your hearing.' "

The Scriptures have as one of their overriding concerns an interest in justice, mercy, and the poor. These matters were of particular concern to the writers of the Old Testament. Time and time again, the Israelites would make sure they kept the religious laws only to ignore pursuing the outcomes the religious laws were designed to preserve.

These concerns are particularly highlighted in the books of Hosea and Amos. The Lord makes clear that His desire is for "mercy, not sacrifice" (Hosea 6:6). He clearly communicates His desire for justice and righteousness as compared with only religious songs, music, religious feasts, and offerings (Amos 5).

Jesus makes many strong statements about His concern for the poor and oppressed. One of His strongest is found in this Luke passage.

At times in the organization it appears that it is easier for us to get more excited about discipleship and evangelism, both at home and abroad, than it is to be excited about the social ramifications of the Christian Gospel. Yet those needs still exist. And we are instructed to attend to them.

LEARNING AND PRACTICING OBEDIENCE

We observed earlier that Jesus learned and practiced obedience. So too must we. Yet obedience demands an object or a principle or a commandment. I can't be obedient to something I don't know about. It is for these reasons that leaders who name the name of Christ must engage in the never-ending process of Bible study—getting to know God better.

A process that has been helpful to me as I have tried to study the Scriptures is to ask three questions about the passages I study. First, according to the passage studied, what is God's desire for the Christian? Second, compared with the biblical expectations stated in the passage, what is my life like? This leads logically to the third question: In order to bring my life into conformity with the Scripture, what has to change? This process of getting to know what God desires of me and then making appropriate changes to make my life conform to His stated desire is for me what growth in Christ involves.

Several years ago I was interviewing a prospective staff member for a position. As is my practice, I asked him to talk to me about his growing commitment to Christ. His answer to me about Christian growth was both simple and profound: giving as much of myself as I know to as much of Christ as I know. That statement illustrates the dynamic of Christian growth. It reflects the reality that I continue to get to know myself better, or at least that should be the case. I also ought to be getting to know Christ better. And once I have accepted Him into my life, as I continue to get to know myself better and as I continue to get to know Him better, I continue to give Him more of me. That process is essential in leadership.

COMPLETE OBEDIENCE

At all costs we must avoid the pitfalls of incomplete or partial obedience. The record of the Scriptures illustrates time after time the results both of obedience and disobedience. We can only conjecture about the results if Noah had decided to build a smaller ark; if Joshua had marched around the walls only three times; if Naaman had dipped into the Jordan River only five times. Moses' incomplete obedience in a limited area cost him dearly. The point, it seems, is clear. Where God has clearly communicated His standard or expectation, He wants complete obedience. Negative consequences are certain for anything less.

Obedience to our Lord is often difficult. Yet it is essential to following and leading.

QUESTIONS FOR FURTHER THOUGHT AND DISCUSSION

1. In what areas are you selectively obedient? Many Christian people fudge regularly with highway speed limits, giving all kinds of rationalizations. Yet how does one who fudges here model obedience for his or her children in other areas?
2. How does the practice of selective obedience in some areas of my life carry over in terms of the way I might be obedient to my Heavenly Father?
3. What's wrong with blind obedience? Does it have any value for a secular government? The military? The kingdom of God?
4. What biblical commands do you find difficult to obey? Why?
5. How do you decide the difference between biblical commandments and biblical suggestions?
6. Do you believe that obedience to the rules is a good thing for an organization? Why or why not?
7. How does one express positive disagreement or dissatisfaction in an organization that puts a premium on obedience to institutional rules?

CHAPTER
SIX

THE LEADER'S NEED TO PRAY

In his provocative article "Tyranny of the Urgent," Charles Hummel quotes P.T. Forsyth as follows: *"The worst sin* is prayerlessness" (emphasis added). Notes Hummel, "We usually think of murder, adultery, or theft as among the worst. But the root of all sin is self-sufficiency—independence from God. When we fail to wait prayerfully for God's guidance and strength we are saying, with our actions if not our lips, that we do not need Him."[1] While we might quarrel with Forsyth's characterization of prayerlessness as the "worst sin," none of us should quarrel with the leader's essential need to be a person of prayer.

Christian leaders of the past have often stated the importance of prayer for the Christian who leads. "Andrew Murray asked, 'What is the reason why many thousands of Christian workers in the world have not a greater influence? Nothing save this—the prayerlessness of their service. . . . It is nothing but the sin of prayerlessness which is the cause of the lack of a powerful spiritual life.' " " 'Great praying,' wrote E.M. Bounds, 'is the sign and seal of God's great leaders. [A leader] must be preeminently a man of prayer. His heart must graduate in the school of prayer. . . . No learning can make up for the failure to pray.' "[2]

Duewel says it this way: "The foundation on which all ministry and leadership is built is your prayer life. Your leadership is never greater than your prayers. Successful leadership requires much more than prayer, but no leadership can ever be ultimately successful apart from much prayer. . . . Other things being equal a praying leader with a praying people will be blessed of God."[3] "Prayer is the basis for whatever ministry one has.·. . . Many Christian leaders' prayer lives are inadequate for the work they are attempting to do."[4] "The apostles . . . decided to give themselves to two things: 'We . . . will give our attention to prayer and the ministry of the word'" (Acts 6:4). Notes Duewel, "You need audience before God before you attempt audience with your people. Stand in God's presence before you stand before them. You must prevail before God before you can prevail before them. Not till you have worshiped with the seraphim are you ready to worship with your people. Only when you come from the presence of God can you lead them into the presence of God."[5]

Richard Foster quotes several people about the importance of prayer for obedient Christians: William Carey: "Prayer—secret, fervent, believing prayer—lies at the root of all personal godliness"[6]; Martin Luther: "I have so much business I cannot get on without spending three hours daily in prayer"[7]; John Wesley: "God does nothing but in answer to prayer."[8] Henri Nouwen observes: "The Christian leader must be in the future what he has always had to be in the past: a man of prayer, a man who has to pray, and who has to pray always. . . . The man of prayer is a leader precisely because through his articulation of God's work within himself he can lead others out of confusion to clarification. . . ."[9]

Regrettably, prayer in the modern world seems to be widely discussed but inadequately practiced. Our personal experiences, if we're honest, probably validate that statement. Again, as Duewel has noted, "Every leader gives lip service to prayer. However, many have a deplorably ineffective prayer life."[10] Knowing of our need for and the importance of prayer, we nevertheless fail to make it a matter of the very highest priority.

James Houston echoes this concern, both within and outside of theological education: "Turn to the index of almost any theological textbook, and it would be a rare moment to discover an entry for 'prayer,' let alone to find a whole chapter in the book on the place of prayer in theological education. . . . Over a century ago, Bishop J.C. Ryle could remark: 'I have come to the conclusion that the vast majority of professing Christians do not pray at all.' Perhaps he would say the same thing of church life in the West today."[11]

Houston makes further observations about the importance of prayer: "In all the areas of our life, prayer is the one where we can least afford to be complacent. We may spend regular times in jogging, exercising and dieting for the sake of our bodies, but refuse to make time for prayer for the sake of our souls. We dedicate enormous effort towards developing our professional skills through expensive education, yet our time and our communion with God has become a lost art and a rejected relationship."[12]

PRAYER DEFINED

Before we proceed further we need to define what we mean by prayer. Leith Samuel has defined prayer this way: "Prayer is not an attempt to change God's mind. Real prayer is communion with God: By it we express our trust in Him, seek to know His mind on the decisions of life, submit to His will, resist in His name the efforts of the devil to frustrate God's loving purposes in human lives." Another has noted this about prayer: "In our communication with God, there must be time for both listening and speaking. God primarily speaks to us through the Scriptures. We speak to God through prayer."[13]

Biehl and Hagelganz also give us some helpful insights on prayer: "In straightforward terms, prayer is simply talking with God—and the simpler the talking, the better. In other words, *prayer is conversation with God*" (emphasis mine).[14] The emphasis is on both conversation (what and how we communicate) and on the triune God (the Person we communicate with). These writers see prayer as consisting of more than words; it is also the "deep expression of the soul."

Biehl and Hagelganz also see *prayer as listening*, "as God talks with you."[15] As such, they suggest that meditation can be an important part of prayer. They suggest further that *prayer is telling God, "So let it be,"* noting that the word *amen* is "really a scriptural word of affirmation in the belief that God has heard our prayer."[16]

The rest of this chapter focuses on the importance of prayer in leadership. We will begin by looking at reasons why prayer is not pursued more diligently. Then we will briefly review what prayer involves, noting particularly the role of prayer in the life of Jesus. We'll also briefly review the practice of prayer as seen elsewhere in the Scripture. We'll close by suggesting how we as leaders might be more involved with personal prayer.

It is important that I note from the start that I write these paragraphs from the perspective of one who has much to learn about prayer and about praying. These words, then, reflect what I am learning about prayer as the Lord continues to teach me.

WHY LEADERS DON'T PRAY

☐ *Prayer as duty or discipline*

Many times prayer is presented as primarily a spiritual discipline or duty, as spiritual drudgery, a kind of spiritual "have to." Observes Houston: "Many people have the impression that prayer is simply another thing we do, alongside all the other activities we pack into our lives. This way of thinking, which sees prayer as an interest or a duty, may prompt us to read about prayer in exactly the same way that we learn from 'how-to' books about cross-country skiing or stamp collecting."[17]

This is also the context, for example, in which Foster presents his helpful discussion on prayer (as we have previously noted). In a similar way, Jerry Bridges sees the practice of godliness as a discipline: "The practice of godliness is an exercise or discipline that focuses upon God."[18] Yet pure discipline, however biblical the concept might be (and I believe it is a biblical concept), is not viewed with much favor when most of the world operates on an "only if and when I feel like it" mentality. People want to be positive and prayer as duty or discipline is seen as a negative concept. Hence prayer simply "doesn't fly" for a lot of Christians.

☐ *Prayer as low priority*

There are so many other spiritual things to do, such as meditating, fasting, and reading the Scripture. There are so many family needs to be met. And then there are the many vocational demands on my daily activities. All of us tend to be busy—most of the time doing good things. And prayer simply becomes one more boat floating on the already crowded sea of busyness, constantly pushed farther and farther away from the harbor of the important things in life.

Yet Houston notes that the Desert Fathers spoke of "busyness as 'moral laziness.'" He writes that "busyness acts to repress our inner fears and personal anxieties, as we scramble to achieve an enviable image to display to others. We become 'outward' people obsessed with how we appear, rather than 'inward' people, reflecting on the meaning of our lives. . . . We define ourselves by what we do, rather than by any quality of what we are inside. . . . Since prayer belongs to the relational side of human life (to 'who I am' rather than to 'what I do'), it is inevitable that prayer will have a very low priority, at the very best, for people who live busy lives. None of us is too busy for the things that we regard as priorities."[19]

If God is concerned about what we *do*, He is even more concerned about who we *are*, on the inside. In His teaching, Jesus repeatedly emphasized "the inner side" of people. He regularly denounced the Pharisees for their preoccupation with the externals (how they appeared to other people) rather than the internals (how they appeared to the Lord):

> You clean the *outside* of the cup and dish, but *inside* they are full of greed and self-indulgence. Blind Pharisee! First clean the *inside* of the cup and dish, and then the *outside* also will be clean. . . . You are like whitewashed tombs, which look beautiful on the *outside* but on the *inside* are full of dead men's bones and everything unclean. In the same way, on the *outside* you appear to people as righteous but on the *inside* you are full of hypocrisy and wickedness (Matthew 23:25-29, emphasis mine).

> Don't you see that whatever enters the mouth goes into the stomach and then out of the body? But the things that come out of the mouth come from the heart, and these make a man "unclean." For out of the heart come evil thoughts, murder, adultery, sexual immorality, theft, false testimony, slander. These are what make a man "unclean" (Matthew 15:17-20).

As we will see, one of the elements which motivates us to make prayer among our highest priorities is the need to understand ourselves from the inside out, not simply as man sees us but as God does. Only then will we more clearly realize our great spiritual need and express our thankfulness to God who loved us so much that He gave His Son for our redemption.

☐ *Prayerlessness as self-centeredness*

In some parts of the world there is an unhealthy emphasis on becoming self-fulfilled and achieving one's potential. This leads to a preoccupation with one's self at great expense to a proper understanding of the individual in community. Self-interest clearly dominates over any sense of common interest. Houston observes that "such a faith drives us all to become Robinson Crusoes, each in our personal desert-island paradise, living according to our own fantasies. . . . Prayerlessness is simply part of a larger picture of modern life, of being alone in a crowd."[20]

Sadly, this independency from others many times carries over into an independency from God. Self-sufficiency and the lordship of Christ are mutually exclusive concepts. While the pursuit of "my potential" may be a worthy goal, its attempted fulfillment outside of my total dependency on Christ will drive me away from an active life of prayer.

☐ *Prayer as a mirror*

Perhaps one of the reasons we don't spend more time in prayer is that when we honestly pray we cannot be involved with charades. Seeing ourselves as God sees us can sometimes frighten us to our very depths. As Houston has noted:

> Knowing ourselves is usually uncomfortable. That is why so many people live inside masks to prevent others discovering the uncomfortable truths they have found out about themselves. Knowing yourself is not flattering. *We often evade what we do not like inside by condemning other people for exactly the same weaknesses.* This is where prayer cuts across all our pretensions. Prayer is the mirror of the soul, and in it we see ourselves most clearly (emphasis mine).[21]

Communicating with the all-knowing God precludes our indulgence with pretense. He sees all that we do and knows our motive for doing it. Coming to Him in prayer requires brutal honesty and openness. And it's our difficulty in so doing that sometimes keeps us from the transforming power of prayer. As we see from James 1:22-25, the Word of God can function as a mirror for us, as long as we honestly respond by doing what we hear and see. Yet many of us either refuse to look into the mirror or we carry away a less than honest picture of what we see. We hate mirrors because they reflect us as we are. And many times we despise what we see. This leads to continued prayerlessness.

PRAYER AS RELATIONSHIP

If there is one overriding observation I would make about prayer, it is this: Prayer flows out of our relationship with the Father, Son, and Holy Spirit. This puts the matter of praying clearly on the side of "want to" or privilege rather than on the side of "have to" or duty. Nothing has transformed my idea of prayer more than this.

To help explain what I mean here, I first want to focus on the relationship which exists between the Father and the Son. For it is in the context of their relationship that we come to understand better Christ's teaching on prayer. Second, we will look at the relationship between the Son and His followers.

1. *Between the Son and the Father. Christ saw Himself as totally dependent on the Father.* Throughout the Book of John, Jesus discusses this relationship:

> I tell you the truth, the Son can do nothing by Himself; He can do only what He sees His Father doing, because whatever the Father does the Son also does (5:19).

> By Myself I can do nothing; I judge only as I hear, and My judgment is just, for I seek not to please Myself but Him who sent Me (5:30).

> My Father, who has given [My sheep] to Me, is greater than all; no one can snatch them out of My Father's hand. I and the Father are one (10:29-30).

> Do not believe Me unless I do what My Father does. But if I do it, even though you do not believe in Me, believe the

miracles, that you may know and understand that the Father is in Me, and I in the Father (10:37-38).

Anyone who has seen Me has seen the Father.... Don't you believe that I am in the Father, and that the Father is in Me? The words I say to you are not just My own. Rather, it is the Father, living in Me, who is doing His work (14:9-10).

These words you hear are not My own; they belong to the Father who sent Me (14:24).

My prayer is not for them alone. I pray also for those who believe, that all of them may be one, Father, just as You are in Me and I am in You. May they also be in Us so that the world may believe that You have sent Me. I have given them the glory that You gave Me, that they may be one as We are one: I in them and You in Me. May they be brought to complete unity to let the world know that You sent Me and have loved them even as You have loved Me (17:20-23).

These verses and many others suggest that *Christ was totally intent on doing the will of His Father* rather than His own. This is probably nowhere better illustrated than in Christ's prayer in Gethsemane, right before He went to the cross. On three separate occasions He pleaded with His Father to be released from drinking the Father's cup. Yet on each occurrence, He clearly submitted His own request to that of the Father's will:

My Father, if it is possible, may this cup be taken from Me. *Yet not as I will, but as You will* (Matthew 26:39, emphasis mine throughout).

My Father, if it is not possible for this cup to be taken away unless I drink it, *may Your will be done* (verse 42).

So He left them and went away once more and prayed the third time, *saying the same thing* (verse 44).

When we see Christ praying to the Father, then, we see the prayer of Persons deeply involved in relationship.

2. *Between the Son and His followers.* In a similar way that Christ and His Father had an intense relationship, *Christ desires that same relationship of those who follow Him*—with us! We see this desire in several ways, first in

terms of a general expectation for believers. When asked by a legal expert which was the greatest commandment in the Law, Jesus responded: "Love the Lord your God with all your heart and with all your soul and with all your mind. This is the first and greatest commandment" (Matthew 22:37-38). Whatever else this verse teaches, it teaches Christ's desire for relationship with us.

Further, not only does He desire relationship with us, he tells us that *apart from Him we will not experience any fruitfulness in our lives:*

> Remain in Me, and I will remain in you. No branch can bear fruit by itself; it must remain in the vine. Neither can you bear fruit unless you remain in Me. I am the vine; you are the branches. If a man remains in Me and I in him, he will bear much fruit; apart from Me you can do nothing (John 15:4-5).

The entire John 15 passage illustrates our need to be in relationship to Christ. He not only desires this relationship; our fruitfulness depends on it.

It is in the context of this relationship, both of Christ to His Father, and of Christ to His people, that I am given the privilege of prayer, of communicating with Him. Communication with Him is not something I have to do; it is something I desire to do. Prayer flows out of my knowledge of His deep love for me and His desire for my fruitfulness. As He changes my heart and transforms my mind (the inner me), prayer changes from a "have to" to a "want to."

PRAYER AS FELLOWSHIP

It follows, then, that if we see prayer as relationship, we also will see prayer as fellowship. We have a tendency in the North American church to see fellowship as a social time among fellow believers, something associated with eating and refreshment. While I believe these may be important parts of Christian fellowship, there is definitely more to it than that.

At a recent Sunday School class, our study group was asked to identify key ways that we fellowship with people. Here are several of the key elements we discussed:

☐ Regular two-way communication, involving talking and listening;

☐ Expressed and genuine interest in another person or persons;

☐ Presence, that is, being physically with others—if possible—rather than settling only for letters and phone calls;

☐ Sharing common meals; and

☐ Sharing joys and burdens.

While fellowship may have other components, these are some of the ways we "fellowship" at the human or horizontal level.

The Scriptures also present a vertical dimension to fellowship. A good illustration of this is found in 1 John 1:3: "We proclaim to you what we have seen and heard, so that you also may have fellowship with us. And our fellowship is with the Father and with His Son, Jesus Christ." Indeed, this verse illustrates both dimensions of fellowship, the horizontal (with people) and the vertical (with the Lord).

In a similar way, then, that we desire fellowship with each other, we pursue fellowship with the Father. He certainly desires this of us. We pursue fellowship in order to sustain our "lives in Christ." And prayer is one of the ways we communicate with and accordingly fellowship with the Father.

JESUS' TEACHINGS ABOUT PRAYER

My intent here is not to provide an inclusive list of the Lord's teachings on prayer, but I do want to explore several key passages, particularly Matthew 6.

According to Matthew's account, Jesus had just finished teaching about how people should love their enemies: "Love your enemies and pray for those who persecute you" (5:44). Jesus then turns to instruction on how people were to pursue acts of righteousness, dealing first with the matter of giving to the needy, then praying, and finally fasting. His general concern seems to be that we not "show off" our acts of righteousness.

On the subject of prayer, He appears to have several concerns. *First,* He specifically cautions against praying in public, to be seen by men. One commentator suggests this represents Christ's concern that we guard against "ostentatiousness" in prayer.[22] Rather, He seems to encourage private prayer ("go into your room, close the door") without embellishment.

Perhaps a positive relationship exists between effectiveness in prayer and solitude. Many would so testify. The Gospels repeatedly note the fact that many of Jesus' prayers were private prayers:

> Very early in the morning, while it was still dark, Jesus got up, left the house and went off to a solitary place, where He prayed (Mark 1:35).

> After leaving them, He went up on a mountainside to pray (Mark 6:46).

> But Jesus often withdrew to lonely places and prayed (Luke 5:16).

> After He had dismissed them, He went up on a mountainside by Himself to pray (Matthew 14:23).

There is a side observation I want to make at this point about solitude. Even though we're discussing solitude in the context of prayer, I am convinced that solitude is also necessary for formation of the leadership vision, something I discussed in my first book. As I spend time in solitude, and in prayer, I believe there is an increased likelihood that God will meet me and confirm in my heart His vision and direction for my life. This comes through listening, through meditating, through reflecting, and through prayer. I like Calvin Miller's thoughts on the relationship between vision and solitude: "God does not shout His best vision through hassled Christian living. It is in quiet that He gives the most delivering visions of life."[23] Prayer and solitude are, it seems to me, mutually related concepts.

Second, Jesus cautions against people "babbling like pagans" in their praying. This same commentator[24] remarks that Christ's concern was for unnecessary "formality" in prayer, noting that the Greek translates "vain repetitions" as to "speak words without thought or meaning."

A *third* concern Christ had about people's prayers was their "lack of trust in their Heavenly Father who knew all their needs."[25] This was another reason, apparently, why there was no need to babble or to use words meaninglessly.

One implication of these preliminary observations about prayer is that our attitude in coming to prayer is critically important. I need to make sure my heart is "clean." As I pray I need to acknowledge the Father as the giver of every good gift. As I pray I must be careful not to use words that I might think will manipulate God into responding favorably to my requests. To do so serves no good purpose because He knows my needs even before I pray.

Now, let's examine a bit more closely Christ's instructions on prayer as found in the Sermon on the Mount, highlighting seven specific guidelines.

1. *We pray to "Our Father"* (Matthew 6:9). While He may be my Father, He is not mine alone. Prayers need to be directed to our Father. Jesus taught elsewhere that the Father is the One who gives us the answer to our requests: "In that day you will no longer ask Me anything. I tell you the truth, My Father will give you whatever you ask in My name" (John 16:23). And when we pray to Him we must recognize His holiness ("hallowed be Your name").

2. *We need to acknowledge the primacy of God's kingdom and ask that His will be done in our lives,* "on earth as it is in heaven" (Matthew 6:10). In brief, whatever we ask must be consistent with His kingdom and His will for us. Too often, we pursue the reverse emphasis, asking that our desires be superimposed on His kingdom. Jesus' teaching illustrates the way He lived His own life: "Yet not as I will, but as You will" (26:40). We need always to align our requests with His will for us.

3. *We start our petitions by asking for our daily bread* (6:11). This instruction clearly allows us to make requests of the Father, here, for our needs *of the day.* Jesus reemphasizes this "daily" focus later on when He tells His hearers: "Therefore do not worry about tomorrow, for tomorrow will worry about itself. Each day has enough trouble of its own" (verse 34).

I am impressed with the "basic essentials" part of Christ's teaching as well as its immediacy. It suggests daily "going to the Father" for the needs of the physical body, as opposed to only once or twice a week or whenever a crisis arises. If we were to store up many months' or even years' worth of what we "need," the process of doing so would drive us away from our daily dependence on Him. As I write this I recall God's similar instruction to the Israelites in Exodus 16 about collecting only enough manna for one day (except for the Sabbath). Jesus' instruction here and other references elsewhere in Scripture suggest a *daily* walk with the Lord, particularly so in this matter of prayer and His interest in our needs.

4. *We are to request our Father to forgive us our debts or sins as we have forgiven others who have sinned against us* (Matthew 6:12). The nature of this request has to do with the spiritual needs rather than physical ones. It has to do not only with the cleanliness of my own heart but also of those I'm involved with in community. This request notes the importance of making sure that I and those I work with serve the Father with clean consciences—such is the Father's will. Later in this same passage Christ underscores the focus on community so strongly that He notes individual forgiveness from the Father is *impossible* if we choose not to forgive others who have sinned against us and who have requested our forgiveness (verses 14-15). The Father wants to make sure we have clean hearts and forgiveness from others *before* we request forgiveness for ourselves from Him.

5. *We should ask the Father to protect and deliver us from the temptations of the evil one* (verse 13). Jesus reminds us that the battles of life involve more than our physical needs (daily bread) or more than making sure we live in proper relationship with others in community. He reminds us that we're involved in a battle for our souls with other spiritual powers. I'm reminded of Paul's words in Ephesians 6:12: "For our struggle is not against flesh and blood, but against the rulers, against the authorities, against the powers of the dark world and against the spiritual forces of evil in the heavenly realms."

6. *We are to come to the Father in Jesus' name.* Though not part of His teaching in the Sermon on the Mount, Christ makes this point repeatedly in the Book of John:

> And I will do whatever you ask in My name, so that the Son may bring glory to the Father. You may ask Me for anything in My name, and I will do it (14:13-14).

You did not choose Me, but I chose you to go and bear fruit—fruit that will last. Then the Father will give you whatever you ask in My name (15:16).

In that day you will no longer ask Me anything. I tell you the truth, My Father will give you whatever you ask in My name (16:23).

7. *We are to be persistent in prayer.* Jesus gives us several examples and I want to look at just two, one in Luke 18 and the other in Matthew 7.

In the Luke 18 passage, right from the beginning Jesus tells us the purpose of the Parable of the Persistent Widow: "to show them [His disciples] that *they should always pray and not give up*" (verse 1, emphasis mine). There are two actors in the story—a widow and a hardhearted judge who neither feared God nor cared about man. As Jesus tells the story, the woman kept coming to the judge with one simple request, "Grant me justice against my adversary" (verse 3). At first the judge refused, but at last he gave in so the widow wouldn't wear him out with her coming (verse 5). Jesus concludes that God is infinitely more patient and merciful than this judge and will certainly grant "justice to His chosen ones, who cry out to Him day and night" (verse 7).

In Matthew 7 Jesus teaches His disciples that when it comes to making requests of the Father, they are to ask, seek, and knock:

Ask and it will be given to you; seek and you will find; knock and the door will be opened to you. For everyone who asks receives; he who seeks finds; and to him who knocks, the door will be opened. Which of you, if his son asks for bread, will give him a stone? Or if he asks for a fish, will he give him a snake? If you, then, though you are evil, know how to give good gifts to your children, how much more will your Father in heaven give good gifts to those who ask Him! (verses 7-11)

Whatever else we learn from these verses, they teach us about persistence in prayer.

SELECTED BIBLICAL EXAMPLES OF PEOPLE WHO PRAYED

Prayer was part and parcel of those who walked with the Lord. For instance, *Samuel* felt such a strong responsibility to pray for his people that he said, "Far be it from me that I should sin against the Lord by failing to pray for you" (1 Samuel 12:23).

There are frequent references in the Psalms to the prayers of *David*, such as this one in Psalm 32:6: "Therefore let everyone who is godly pray to You while You may be found."

Probably one of the best known people of prayer in the Old Testament is *Daniel.* It was said of him, "Three times a day he got down on his knees and prayed, giving thanks to his God" (Daniel 6:10). Why are we not surprised to read about Daniel what ought to be the goal of every person who names the name of Christ, especially leaders: "Daniel ... distinguished himself among the administrators and the satraps by his exceptional qualities. ... They [Daniel's accusers] could find no corruption in him, because he was trustworthy and neither corrupt nor negligent" (verses 3-4). Prayer and righteousness in the sight of God seem to be inextricably related.

What about New Testament examples? There are many references to prayer throughout the Book of Acts. In chapter 1 we read that the disciples "all joined together constantly in prayer" (verse 14). As the church grew, some set themselves apart to the ministry of prayer (2:42). In times of distress, voices were raised together in prayer (4:24-31). Chapter 6 notes that the Twelve devoted themselves to prayer and the ministry of the Word (verse 4). Fasting and prayer are linked in 13:3. And later we find Paul and Silas in jail praying and singing (16:25). Simply put, the early church was consumed by its need for prayer.

Throughout the writings of Paul, he notes his commitment to prayer and encourages others to pray. He tells us to: be faithful in prayer (Romans 12:12); present our requests in prayer and petition (Philippians 4:6); devote ourselves to prayer (Colossians 4:2); lift up holy hands in prayer (1 Timothy 2:8); and pray continually (1 Thessalonians 5:17). He frequently noted that he prayed regularly for the recipients of his letters (Colossians 1:9-10; 2 Thessalonians 1:11) and regularly requested prayer for himself (Colossians 4:3).

James exhorted people in trouble and the sick to pray (James 5:13-16). *Peter* reminded his readers that they were to be clear-minded and self-controlled, so they could pray (1 Peter 4:7). *Jude* instructed his readers to pray in the Holy Spirit (Jude 20). In this same way, *Paul* reminded us that when we don't know what to pray, "the Spirit Himself intercedes for us with groans that words cannot express" (Romans 8:26).

PRACTICAL SUGGESTIONS ABOUT PRAYING

Having previously made the observation that prayer is communication with God and that communication with Him is enhanced by relationship and fellowship, I now turn to some practical suggestions about how we might approach God in prayer.

Earlier in our Christian walk, my wife Marylou and I learned to pray following the ACTS guideline. While we profess no expertise in praying, we found ACTS helpful to get us started.

☐ The "A" stands for *adoration*.
☐ The "C" represents *confession*.
☐ The "T" represents *thanksgiving*.
☐ The "S" stands for *supplication*.

We begin our prayer with adoration of the Father, talking about His greatness and His glory. Thereafter, we move to confession of sin. Next, we praise and thank God for all that He has done and continues to do for us. Finally, we make requests of the Father. Interestingly, each of the four steps is included in the model prayer Jesus taught His disciples. While this approach to prayer may seem simplistic, I don't intend for it to be so. Nor will I suggest amounts of time for each phase.

Biehl and Hagelganz suggest many helpful guidelines in their book *Praying*. For example, I really like their emphasis on prayer as listening to God: "There should be times when you relax completely, put everything out of your mind, and allow God to speak. This is a time for recreation—for renewal. To pour out your heart to God is important; but let God pour Himself into you as well."[26] Biehl identifies meditation (see, for example, Psalm 1:2 and Joshua 1:8) as one of the ways we listen to God: "Actually, meditation is a form of prayer. We usually think of prayer as our talking to God through praise, petition, intercession, thanksgiving, and confession. I like to think of meditation as the 'other side' of prayer—the listening side."[27]

When I read and study the Scriptures, I need to do a better job of taking some time immediately afterward to let God, through the Holy Spirit, speak to me about what I just read. As we already noted, God speaks to us through the Scripture. We need to take time to listen to His voice, after which follow-up communication with the Father may ensue. Prayer in this way, then, is listening to and communicating with the Father through the Scripture. Some have suggested that this kind of prayer ought to *precede* other kinds of praying, such as our use of prayer lists and making requests. Interestingly, Jesus taught His disciples in His model prayer the importance of praying for the Father's will before making requests to the Father.

In addition to prayer as talking and listening, Biehl and Hagelganz identify similar elements of prayer represented in our ACTS guideline. They do, however, make one important addition. They follow supplication (petition) with intercession. Intercession is praying for another need totally outside of and beyond my own needs. When I pray for others or other organizations, I'm involved with intercession.

Probably one of the great examples of intercessory prayer is the prayer of Jesus in John 17:20: "My prayer is not for them alone. I pray also for those who will believe in Me through their message." Intercessory prayer drives me to see God's world—the big picture, if you will—rather than being preoccupied with only my miniscule part of it.

I see *prayer lists* as important parts of the request or petition side of prayer. Categorizing requests by areas such as family, church, work, missions, and government; noting dates the specific request was made, followed by the date the prayer was answered, and then filing those answers for future reference provides a historical reminder of the way

God has particularly involved Himself with my life and the lives of others.

Finally, I argue for *prayer particularly in the morning*. I am well aware that the Scriptures note people praying at a variety of times throughout the day and night. Daniel and our Lord are but two examples. Alternatively, I believe praying in the morning, after a good night's rest and before the business of the day clouds the mind, is a time when prayer can be particularly effective. We do know from the Psalms (see, for example, 5:3) that the morning was one of David's favorite times for prayer.

CONCLUSION

I can't argue strongly enough that prayer is an important part of biblical discipleship. And it is critically important for leadership. Duewel quotes E.M. Bounds here:

> [Each leader] must be preeminently a man of prayer. . . . No learning can make up for the failure to pray. No earnestness, no diligence, no study, no gifts will supply its lack. Talking to men for God is a great thing, but talking to God for men is greater still. He will never talk well and with real success to men for God who has not learned well how to talk to God for men.[28]

As Duewel also observes, "You will never be a greater leader than your prayers."[29]

"Father in Heaven, in the name of Your Son, Jesus, help us to be men and women of prayer in our leading and following. Amen."

QUESTIONS FOR FURTHER THOUGHT AND DISCUSSION

1. What time of the day have you found to be best for sustained prayer?
2. What do you believe the Scripture means in 1 Thessalonians 5:17 to "pray continually"?
3. Does effective prayer require any special prayer position? What about a special prayer vocabulary?

4. What are some of the ways you teach prayer to your family? For example, for many years my wife and I had found it difficult to pray together. We found our experience mirrored by many other couples. Why do you think that is the case?
5. Do you feel comfortable being called on without advance notice to pray in church or some other public meeting? Why or why not?
6. When given an "assignment" to pray in public, is it wrong to write out a prayer in advance? Must all prayer be spontaneous?

PERSONAL RENEWAL IN LEADERSHIP

In this chapter we want to look at personal renewal in leadership. In particular, I want to discuss the subject of the Sabbath as a potential key to personal renewal. We also want to study the Prophet Elijah to see how God dealt with him on this issue.

The Bible offers numerous examples that help inform our perspective on personal renewal. Paul had as a driving concern a desire for spiritual renewal. He desired that those who knew Christ would be transformed by the renewing of their minds (Romans 12:2). Paul knew that being committed to Christ would change the way people lived. And the rest of Romans 12 spells out some of the evidences of spiritual renewal.

REASONS WE NEED RENEWAL

If we were to list danger points in contemporary Christian leadership, inattention to personal renewal would come very high on the list. For many leaders, the norm would probably look like this: neglected family priorities, neglected physical fitness priorities, and neglected spiritual priorities. I have talked with enough people in organizational leadership to know that this is a monumental problem. Few leaders will lay on their death bed wishing they had spent more time in the office and less time with their families. Fewer still will be able to identify with Paul's statement that he stayed the course of his calling. We all know of our need for renewal, yet we neglect it. Why? Better yet, why do we have these concerns for personal renewal in the first place?

John Gardner in his classic *Self-Renewal* suggests that we all stagnate as people if we don't involve ourselves in activities of renewal:

> "Keep on growing," the commencement speakers say. "Don't go to seed. Let this be a beginning, not an ending." It is a good theme. Yet a high proportion of the young people who hear the speeches pay no heed, and by the time they are middle-aged they are absolutely mummified. As we mature we progressively narrow the scope and variety of our lives. . . . We become caught in a web of fixed relationships. We develop set ways of doing things. . . . The most stubborn protector of his own vested interest is the man who has lost the capacity for self-renewal.[1]

Personal experience affirms Gardner's observations.

We need to be pursuing personal renewal because some would say that leadership is tougher now than in earlier generations. They argue that the complexity of the leadership challenge is continuing to accelerate. A recent comment by Harvard professor John Kotter illustrates this view. Addressing the personal requirements needed for leaders, he states: "Even in the simplest conditions a variety of things are needed to create the vision and strategy, and to elicit the teamwork and motivation. *But simple conditions are not the norm any more. Complexity is the norm*" (emphasis mine).[2] He then notes the varying degrees of incremental complexity given the nature of the organization, the number and kind of people involved, and the technology used.

Further, longevity in a significant position of organizational leadership, whether as pastor of a church, president of a college, or head coach of an athletic team, tends to be the exception, rather than the rule. Kotter observes that one of the key ingredients in effective leadership is "a tremendous energy level and a deep desire to use that energy for supplying leadership."[3] Anyone who has held or who holds such a position of leadership knows the need for high energy. A tired or exhausted leader will rarely be effective.

FACTORS WHICH PREVENT RENEWAL

Why do we leaders in organizations struggle so much with personal renewal? *First*, there is the press of our egos. No leader wants to fail or to be involved with what Kets de Vries calls the "F-dimension (failure factor)."[4] So all of our personal time and energy are spent on the organizational agenda and its health rather than incorporating and merging together our personal and family agenda. While personal family failures become more and more acceptable in society, few leaders want it to be said of them, "And the organization 'went under' during his/her administration." Every leader wants to be seen as deserving the trust of the organization.

In spite of religious rhetoric such as "God has called me elsewhere," leaders look for the right opportunity to leave "failing" organizations. Few leave thriving enterprises that are financially solid and spiritually sound. People want to be part of a "winner." Leaders are no different. And many are driven by ego to make sure their organization stays or becomes a "winner." Many do so at great personal and physical cost. Many leave their organization hoping naively that a change of scenery, problems, and people will help them become renewed.

Second, one of the unspoken rules in an organization is that enough is never enough. If the organization is a church, a better and bigger building, more programs, more staff, and, obviously, more money are needed. The same can be said about almost any other kind of Christian organization. We assert our belief in a God who claims He is capable of meeting our needs. Yet why is it that we always need more? Does Christian theology ever permit organizations to ask and indeed settle for less?

Christian leaders pick up on this "but more is needed" philosophy and become enslaved to it. Since there are so many lost souls out there I must always say yes to invitations to speak. Since money is always needed, I must make all the fund-raising calls I can. I must get into as many churches or homes as I can. Church families need me; staff need me; students need me; donors need me, and so the list continues. Pastors and other leaders willingly spend this time for the organizations they serve, knowing the shepherd is to lay down his life for the sheep. The extreme needs of the church "justify" less attention to family needs. As one writer has put it, "You as the leader have such a heavy responsibility of daily prayer for your people that you may have to limit the amount of time you pray for yourself and your own family."[5]

The press of the job is a *third* reason for personal burnout. Leadership responsibilities have become more complex. More time is needed just to stay on top of the job. One of the practices I had followed for years was going to the office on Saturday mornings to do creative work—to write and to dream. Yet in recent years I remember telling my wife Marylou that I now go to the office in the mornings and evenings just to stay caught up and out of a sense of obligation to do so. Many leaders can identify with this sense of being consumed by the job. And the danger from this can be deadly when the work holds a high enjoyment level.

A *fourth* reason we fail to pursue personal renewal is that we have a seemingly built-in drive for promotion and prestige. We become uncomfortable with our "current situation in life" and therefore want to "minister" at a bigger church, a bigger college, or a bigger organization. We want the prestige that comes from working somewhere (anywhere other than where we are) that the secular world thinks is a "big deal." And we know that we won't be recognized for our achievements (by another organization elsewhere) if we don't overachieve in our current position. So we work excessive hours to try to prove to others that we deserve to be given a chance at a better position.

This attitude, and all of us have battled it at one time or another, ignores the biblical teaching that our work is always done for the Lord, not for an organization. John also cautions us about a preoccupation with "the pride of life" or the "boastings of what he has and does." Such thoughts come "not from the Father but from the world" (1 John 2:16).

One of the best stories I have heard on this topic was told by a veteran missionary who protested the fact that God had called him to the mission field, and apparently into seeming oblivion, while all of his friends back home were "achieving" more important and "recognizable" things. As this dear saint listened for God's answer to his tired protest, the response that he heard from the Lord was something like this: "My son, *your* responsibility is to concern yourself with the depth [what God thinks of you] of your walk with Me. It is *My* responsibility to handle the breadth [what man thinks of you] of your walk with Me." King David said it this way: "In Your hands are strength and power to exalt and give strength to all" (1 Chronicles 29:12). Simply put, a selfish desire for promotion and recognition and the false need to keep proving yourself to others are seldom if ever excuses to ignore personal renewal.

THE SABBATH AND PERSONAL RENEWAL

While trying to avoid being simplistic in an effort to address this concern for personal renewal, I believe one significant way of dealing with its necessity can be found in the concept of the Sabbath. One of the Ten Commandments, the Sabbath is a concept Jesus practiced and appeared to both honor and accept (though not necessarily all the legalistic requirements that people had added to it).

Without trying to be legalistic about it, many of us grew up in an evangelical era that gave little attention to the Sabbath. Other than infrequent references to the fact that Sunday needed to be different, one back then and probably still today heard little about this important biblical concept. After all, the "Sabbath" is an Old Testament concept given under Law, and modern, enlightened Christians are under grace. But let's look at it a bit more carefully, for the Scripture (only a small number of illustrative verses will be referred to here) presents the Sabbath as having several important goals that we ought to consider.

☐ *The Sabbath as a day of rest*

The idea of the Sabbath as a *day* of rest comes to us early in Scripture for we read in Genesis 2:2-3:

> By the seventh day God had finished the work He had been doing; so on the seventh day He rested from all His work. And God blessed the seventh day and made it holy, because on it He rested from all the work of creating that He had done.

We don't know why God rested. It was obviously not because He was tired and burned out. But He rested on the seventh day; He blessed the seventh day; and He made it holy. So we know from the beginning of Creation that the seventh day is to be different based on what God Himself says about it.

This day-of-rest concept begins to acquire additional meaning in verses like Exodus 20:8, 23:12, 34:21, and 35:1-3. In the first instance—as part of the Ten Commandments—the instruction comes to us that the people are to labor and to do all of their work in six days. This applied to families, servants, and to animals as well. The reason for this commandment appears to be God's example in resting on the seventh day of Creation. Exodus 23:12 suggests rest and refreshment both for people and animals as being one of the results of the Sabbath: "Six days do your work, but on the seventh day do not work, so that your ox and your donkey may rest and the slave born in your household, and the alien as well, may be refreshed." In this regard I would note that while refreshment may not be the sole purpose of the Sabbath, it is at least one of the purposes for it.

Additional Scriptures (here I have in mind verses like Exodus 31:12-14 and Leviticus 23:3) expand the significance of the Sabbath Day concept to include the covenant God made between Himself and the people. The reference in Leviticus includes the idea of it being a "day of sacred assembly."

For our limited purposes I want to highlight only the rest and refreshment aspects of the Sabbath Day. Whatever else may be its significance, one main purpose of the Sabbath is that once every seven days there ought not be any work done of the type one normally does the other six days. Outcomes of the day include rest (both personal and corporate), refreshment, and sacred assembly before the Lord. A significant number of contemporary believers choose Sunday as their "Sabbath" day.

Why is it that sometimes I dread Sundays? Probably because sometimes Sunday is a day of exhaustion. Invitations to speak at churches often take me away from my family the whole day (as well as away from our local church) and often the Saturday night before if the church is some distance away. Usually, when I'm at home, the local church has pre-church and post-church meetings as well as Sunday evening services. I value these opportunities to get together on Sundays to praise and worship God. My only caution is that sometimes the busyness of the church day fails to serve the purposes for which God made it.

I am not prepared to make a long list of suggestions about Sabbath Day activity other than to note that as I approach my Sabbath, I need to have answers for questions about how I will spend my time during that day, questions such as: Will what we have planned for our family produce rest and refreshment for us? Will our plans include seeing this day as holy to the Lord (I don't intend to suggest here that other days ought not be holy or further suggest a secular/sacred dichotomy) and as a day of blessing? How will we address the need for sacred assembly? How will we make sure we will not be doing "work" normally done on the previous six days of the week on this one? As I have wrestled with such questions, I have cut back on outside Sunday speaking engagements at other churches and have enjoyed being home with my family in our local church on Sundays. Taking the Sabbath more seriously has been a very positive source of personal renewal for our family.

☐ *The Sabbath as a year of rest*

The Scripture also presents the concept of Sabbath as a *year* of rest for the land. We see this in passages like Leviticus 25:1-7, particularly verses 4 and 5: "But in the seventh year the land is to have a sabbath of rest, a sabbath to the Lord. Do not sow your fields or prune your vineyards. Do not reap what grows of itself or harvest the grapes of your unattended vines. The land is to have a year of rest."

God gave these commands to the Israelites as they looked forward to going into and caring for the Promised Land. Interestingly, those involved with agriculture today likewise talk about the need to rest the land and to rotate crops. Further, we don't know how following this commandment altered the people's lifestyles during this year of rest for the land. Presumably they still did work, but not in the fields. Perhaps they rebuilt their houses. Perhaps equipment was repaired and new clothes were made. It is not farfetched to suggest that, at a minimum, the sabbatical year for the land changed people's routines, work habits, and schedules.

Again, I'm not prepared to make a long list of suggestions as to how this might have relevance, if any, to our discussion about personal renewal. However, I have discussed this matter with enough people to know that significant periods of time, whether one month or several, or indeed up to one year, away from the regular work habit, schedule, and routine can play a very significant part in personal renewal. Aside from all of the many job-related benefits, giving people "sabbaticals" provides opportunities for reflective thinking that otherwise is not possible or probable in the usual routine. A sabbatical provides enhanced opportunities for stillness (see Psalm 46:10), quietness, and heightened spiritual awareness.

The education profession in many parts of the world probably does a better job at providing opportunities for personal renewal than do other professions. "Time off" during the summer provides for changes in routine and schedule. Many educational organizations provide time off through a "sabbatical" program after a requisite number of years of service. As I write this book I am the beneficiary of just such a sabbatical.

Some countries take this "time off" for renewal with great seriousness. During a trip to Australia, I was interested to learn that, as a matter of public practice, if not policy, persons who have been employed for approximately ten years by the same employer are usually given three months off, fully paid, as a "long service leave" benefit.

I believe as Christians we need to address more completely the matter of personal renewal through sabbaticals. I am not arguing for a specific length of sabbatical. What I am suggesting is that the concept of the Sabbath in the Scripture (and I haven't mentioned the related concept of the "year of Jubilee" set forth in Leviticus 25:8-55), both with regard to the "day" and the "year" gives strong biblical precedent for "time off" to be involved with a different routine as necessary for rest and refreshment. Yet if those in positions of leadership don't believe this is important or take personal renewal seriously, then for certain, neither will the people "being led."

Numerous references in the Gospels give evidence to the fact that Jesus often took time off from a very busy schedule to go to a solitary place to be with His Father. Sometimes He took His disciples with Him. Note the following: "They withdrew" (Luke 9:10); "Jesus went out to a mountainside to pray" (6:12); "At daybreak Jesus went out to a solitary place" (4:42); and "But Jesus often withdrew to lonely places and prayed" (5:16). Interestingly, Jesus was so focused in His ministry that even though it lasted little more than three years He could say with confidence to the Father that He had completed the work the Father had sent Him to do (John 17:4). Yet never in the Gospels do we see a "rushed" Jesus.

ELIJAH AND PERSONAL RENEWAL

First Kings tells us much about the life and ministry of Elijah. Israel's King Ahab and his pagan wife, Jezebel, greatly disliked Elijah and were particularly upset with him because of a massive drought in the land, which Elijah had foretold. While the drought was God-sent, the king and queen blamed Elijah for it. As you might imagine, Elijah did a lot of hiding during these days (17:1-3).

Next in the chronology is Elijah's confrontation with the prophets of Baal. This is the story, you'll recall, where he had all the prophets of Baal assemble on Mount Carmel. Then he built an altar, placed a sacrifice on it, and told the people that the god who provided fire to burn the sacrifice—"He is God" (18:24). The people and Baal's prophets agreed to the test. The Baal prophets had first chance—from morning till noon, until the time for the evening sacrifice—for their god to demonstrate his power, all without success. Then Elijah, after having soaked the altar with water, called down fire from heaven. God responded in great power, and the sacrifice was totally consumed. Elijah had all of the prophets of Baal seized and then killed in the Kishon Valley. Shortly thereafter, Elijah prayed for rain, and again God responded, thus ending the drought. But Queen Jezebel, having learned of the death of the prophets of Baal, issued an immediate death warrant for Elijah.

When we find Elijah next, he is one discouraged leader. In spite of all his faithful service for the Lord, in spite of his tremendous spiritual victories, we find this scene: "He came to a broom tree, sat down under it and prayed that he might die. 'I have had enough, Lord,' he said. 'Take my life; I am no better than my ancestors.' Then he lay down under the tree and fell asleep" (19:4-5). At this point Elijah is so downhearted, burnt out, defeated, that he no longer wants to think about living. All he wants to do is die. He has had enough. He is filled with self-pity.

Many leaders at one time or another have experienced Elijah's frustration. Many leaders have said out loud or in their minds: "I quit; I resign; I can't take it anymore; let me out of here." I know I have done so. From almost every perspective, discouragement in leadership is deadly. I find it interesting that at the moment of some of his greatest victories, Elijah appears to be the most defeated. He wanted to quit.

As I have observed persons in leadership roles and as I have reflected on my experience in leadership, some of the most discouraging moments have come immediately after some of the greatest victories. Why is that? Perhaps we are tempted to assume that a significant victory (which usually resulted from a major battle of some sort) means that we'll face no future challenges of significance, at least not for awhile. Perhaps victories tend to make us vulnerable to feelings of pride and less than accurate assessments of our self-worth. Perhaps we think, "If I can do this, I can do anything." Perhaps we are physically so exhausted from one battle that we are unable to handle the next one we see looming on the horizon.

First Kings 19 identifies some of the ways God nursed Elijah back into His service. I want to look at several of them.

1. *Elijah rested* (verse 5). Given the fact that he had just finished a long trip, perhaps walking and running, he was probably tired. Sometimes a good night's rest has a way of providing a new perspective to an old dilemma. Tiredness and effective leadership tend for the most part to be mutually exclusive concepts.

2. *Elijah was given food* (verses 5-8). It would appear

that while he was sleeping, or at least while resting, an angel told him to get up and eat. The angel presumably had provided him with a cake of bread and water. Elijah ate, drank, and then went back to sleep again ("he . . . then lay down again"). Once more, the angel told him to get up and to eat and drink. Elijah did so. And then the angel told Elijah that he needed strength for a long journey. The text states that Elijah was "strengthened by that food." We all know the key role that good food and proper eating habits play in keeping our bodies in good shape.

3. *Elijah was given an assignment that involved strenuous physical exercise* (verses 8-9). He had no visible and presumably no public ministry for at least the next forty days as he "traveled . . . until he reached Horeb, the mountain of God." God literally told Elijah to take a hike. Perhaps more of us need to be hikers. I've often wondered what Elijah thought about as he walked or jogged or ran to Horeb: "Will God still use me? Where am I ever going to get the courage and strength to do this?"

Good reasons for persons to participate in some type of exercise are numerous. Endurance is increased; the ability to think more clearly is improved. Research indicates the connection between good physical condition and enhanced intellectual or cognitive performance. Further, if my experience is common, I know of many people who have very significant communion with God when they're out walking or running. Exercise not only provides physical fitness but it also serves as a way to "center in" on spiritual priorities. Perhaps this was one of the tools God was using for Elijah.

4. *God put Elijah geographically into a new position to experience God in a fresh way.* Sometimes that's true for us as well. Maybe we need to relocate for a short period of time; maybe attend a Bible conference somewhere. In short, maybe we need a change of scenery and a release from our normal environment to experience God in a renewed and powerful way.

5. *Elijah was put into a position of experiencing extended solitude.* Elijah was alone for at least forty days and nights, perhaps longer. When he got to the mountain, he went into a cave. Only after he had been alone for this

extended time did God speak to him. Again, the depth of Elijah's despair and self-pity is evident in his first conversation with God—"I am the only one left" (verse 10). God's response was that Elijah needed to stand in His presence. I find this instruction incredibly powerful. In leadership of any kind, I need to stand in the presence of the Lord. Being alone in God's presence will make a significant difference in the way I lead.

As Elijah waited on the Lord, he observed, in order, a mighty wind, an earthquake, a fire, and then a gentle whisper. God was not in any of the first three but He apparently was in the fourth (verses 11-12). And out of this gentle whisper Elijah heard anew the voice of God along with instructions for his continued service. Solitude, holy stillness, in the presence of the Lord. This was critical to the process used by God for Elijah's restoration. For leaders and others it still is.

THE NEW TESTAMENT CONCEPT OF REST

Jesus urges His disciples in Matthew 11:28-30: "Come to Me, all you who are weary and burdened, and I will give you rest. Take My yoke upon you and learn from Me, for I am gentle and humble in heart, and you will find rest for your souls. For My yoke is easy and My burden is light." Additional key references to "rest" are found in the Book of Hebrews, particularly chapters 3 and 4.

The meanings appear to be severalfold. *First*, there is the idea of spiritual rest as God's true salvation is compared with the false religion and burdens of the Pharisees. Knowing God provides a rest for our souls that can't be satisfied by things or money, power or prestige, or mere religious practices.

Second, there is the idea of rest as a daily resting in Christ; as I give my burdens to Him, He gives me rest. As I hide myself in the God of creation, my perspective changes and so too does my life. This kind of rest doesn't mean we simply stop our work and rest. Rather, it's part of the process of casting our cares on Him and learning from Him, knowing He cares for us. This kind of spiritual rest restores our souls and our minds.

Third, the idea of rest includes the idea of cessation

of normal activities and refocusing our time and energies more intently on the living God. This is in part the kind of rest associated with the Sabbath we talked about earlier. It provides spiritual *and* physical refreshment.

CONCLUSION

During a class at Regent College on the Book of Mark, Professor Michael Green was discussing Mark 6:30-32, verses dealing with the disciples' return after having been sent out by Jesus:

> The apostles gathered around Jesus and reported to Him all they had done and taught. Then, because so many people were coming and going that they did not even have a chance to eat, He said to them, "Come with Me by yourselves to a quiet place and get some rest." So they went away by themselves in a boat to a solitary place.

Professor Green noted that in these three verses we are given insight on how we can avoid burnout. First, the disciples told Jesus everything, something Jesus still desires of us. Then, we see shared leadership. Not only did Jesus share His load, but He sent them out by twos. And third, when the pace got too hectic, He took them to a solitary place—away from the people—to get some rest.

God desires workers and leaders who are personally refreshed and renewed. Obedient practice to what Jesus Himself modeled in this area will do much to help us in our ongoing pursuit of personal renewal.

QUESTIONS FOR FURTHER THOUGHT AND DISCUSSION

1. Do you share the sense of many that we don't pursue personal renewal as aggressively as we should? Why do you think that we tend to struggle in this area?
2. What are some of the ways you think you might be in a rut, where you've become "a protector of your own vested interest"?
3. How do you pursue personal renewal in your own life? If married, do you and your spouse grow or pursue renewal together, or is it more one-sided?

4. Does the way you spend your Sundays contribute to a sense of renewal? How so? If not, what changes do you need to make?

5. Take a few minutes to respond to some of the questions posed in the sections dealing with the Sabbath. Will what you have planned for Sunday produce rest and refreshment for you and your family? How will you as a family address the need for sacred assembly?

6. If you were asked to discuss qualitatively how you spend your vacation, what words would you use? A break from work? Time for refreshment? An opportunity for quality family time? A time to repair the house and to do extra home chores? I remain convinced that the quality of our time to renew, whether through vacations or otherwise, will directly impact the quality of our lives.

CHAPTER
EIGHT

SPIRITUAL RESTORATION, REVIVAL, AND LEADERSHIP

Just what is spiritual restoration and is it connected in any way to a leader's personal renewal? How do leaders "bring" revival, if they do? These are the questions we'll attempt to answer in this chapter.

From a variety of perspectives I see a close relationship between personal renewal and spiritual restoration. While we can do much to prepare the way for both, personal renewal and revival (throughout the balance of this discussion I will use the terms *spiritual restoration* and *revival* interchangeably) ultimately are the results of the Spirit of God at work in us, producing the kind of fruit He desires. I remain convinced, however, that personal renewal can do much to make revival possible.

For example, all of us tend to get captured by the routine of the ordinary. Major changes in our lives, however, produce a context where positive change can occur: "It is not unusual to find that the major changes in life—marriage, a move to a new city, a change of jobs ... break the pattern of our lives and reveal to us quite suddenly how much we had been imprisoned by the comfortable web we had woven around ourselves. . . . We don't know that we've been imprisoned until after we've broken out."[1] It is at times like these that we are ripe for spiritual restoration and revival.

A dictionary definition of the word *revival* suggests that it is a "special effort with meetings, etc., to promote reawakening of religious fervor." The idea of revive is to "bring back . . . to life." There is a sense that religious fervor or life was once present, is now absent, and that revival serves to restore to what once was. In this sense revival is a broad concept. But as we will use the term, we will limit its use primarily to the spiritual domain.

OUR NEED FOR SPIRITUAL RESTORATION AND REVIVAL

I know of few leaders in Christian organizations who are not in need of revival. I know of few Christian organizations (by this I mean the people within them) who would not benefit from revival. All who know Christ should desire to live the way Christ desires them to live. While many of us initially concur with this observation, we may ultimately have some reservations about getting too serious about revival, because we're not sure what God will ask us to do. Spiritual restoration can be quite risky.

Nonetheless, *our Lord has a strong interest in revival or spiritual restoration.* Nowhere can I find a passage of Scripture where God is indifferent to a person's spiritual condition. Rather, we see a God who is actively at work drawing people to Himself both for fellowship and service. His priorities for us seem to be first godliness and then work which results in His receiving glory. He wants new life and growth, constantly pruning to produce it. If necessary, He can bring dry bones back to life (Ezekiel 37) to achieve His purposes. He wants both holy living and unity to be reflected among believers. He wants holy living because it reflects His character; He wants unity in order to demonstrate on earth what is true in heaven (John 17:23; Romans 15:5-6; Psalm 133; Philippians 2:1-2).

Second, *our Lord knows that we will not be able to achieve His agenda, either corporately or individually, without our being part of the living, fruit-bearing Vine.* As Jesus Himself said, "Apart from Me you can do nothing" (John 15:5).

Third, *God wants people of godly character.* He is preoccupied with the unseen things while we tend to focus only on those things which can be seen by others. What's more, we are never completely successful in covering up those unseen things. Each of us has a storage bin in his or her heart; God knows its contents and its overflow will eventually become known to others. As the Scripture says, "The good man brings good things out of the good stored up in his heart, and the evil man brings evil things out of the evil stored up in his heart. For out of the overflow of his heart his mouth speaks" (Luke 6:45). As our Creator, the Lord is a discerner and judge of "the thoughts and attitudes of the heart" (Hebrews 4:12).

Fourth, *He wants obedient people who will be faithful models and messengers of the need for revival.* In this regard I think of Jonah and merely note several key elements of his story. God wanted Jonah to be (1) an obedient servant, (2) who was willing to share a message of good news, (3) to a hostile audience. Further, (4) Jonah's failure to deliver the message would have negative consequences for not only the intended audience but for the reluctant messenger as well.

On several occasions elsewhere in Scripture, God makes it clear that He's serious about extending judgment to a reluctant messenger. Note, for example, His instructions to Ezekiel:

> When I say to a wicked man, "You will surely die," and you do not warn him or speak out to dissuade him from his evil ways in order to save his life, that wicked man will die for his sin and I will hold you accountable for his blood. But if you do warn the wicked man and he does not turn from his wickedness or from his evil ways, he will die for his sin; but you will have saved yourself (Ezekiel 3:18-19).

Interestingly, Jonah needed to be prepared for the results of revival. As you may recall, he became upset when the people of Nineveh repented and God spared them. Are we so different? Are we really prepared for the changes in our churches that revival would bring? What would happen to local church politics and polity if suddenly as a result of our "fire" for God, 3,000 people were added to our local church as happened in Acts 2? Are we really prepared for the changes that revival would make in our personal lives? Would we be prepared for a change of job or lifestyle or a major shift in our priorities that God might direct us to make? Perhaps we're not, and that's why we don't earnestly pray or prepare for it. We're not sure we could handle the changes which might result. "O God, spare us from this apathy and complacency of not wanting Your very best for us."

Another Old Testament example of personal revival is Ezra. After Ezra was released from Babylonian captivity and returned to Jerusalem, he "devoted himself to the study and observance of the Law of the Lord, and to teaching its decrees and laws in Israel" (Ezra 7:10). I find it interesting that the text notes that his first step was *to devote himself for service.* I like the *King James* rendition: "For Ezra had prepared his heart." This action preceded all of his subsequent efforts. And with this "prepared heart" Ezra then sought (2) *to discover the meaning of God's Word;* (3) *to do what he discovered;* and then (4) *to teach others what he had learned.* Note again the chronology: preparation of the heart followed by careful study followed by obedience. Is it any surprise that God honored Ezra's efforts of teaching others about Him?

Some of you are reading this and may be wondering, "What's the big deal?" The big deal, it seems to me, is to realize that revival seldom comes without an emphasis on *holy individual living* which is then coupled with *holy corporate living.* Revival requires that we deal with sin, both individually and corporately. As I write these words, God has burned them indelibly into my heart. He is driving me to new levels of personal integrity in areas of my life where I have been somewhat sloppy. I am learning anew and in very painful ways that a holy God and toleration of sin, of any kind, are mutually exclusive concepts. None of us can presume to ask for or seek His blessing on our lives until we deal with sin.

EVANGELICAL SIN LISTS

One curse of contemporary evangelicalism is that we have developed acceptable and unacceptable sin lists. Socially acceptable sins include pride, divisiveness, gossip, and the like, while socially unacceptable sins include alcohol abuse and drug addiction. Often our lists of "sins" represent a rapidly decreasing ledger of do's and don'ts. Why is it that some people feel more comfortable "pushing the limits" about all the things they can do and still be a Christian rather than pursuing those actions that "honor Him the most"? I say this knowing I myself have sometimes been guilty of just such a mindset.

Another problem with sin lists is that they cause us to focus on the list rather than on the holiness of God. The writer of Hebrews notes that it is the spiritually mature who have learned to discern between good and evil (5:14). Yet given their nature, lists don't require much spiritual discernment. Unfortunately, and as Elisabeth Elliot observes, "thus saith the board" sometimes acquires a higher Christian cultural value than "thus saith the Lord." Might it be that our spiritual legalism, and its usual companion sin lists, have driven us away from godliness because we have exchanged compliance with a list for godly holiness?

John White and Ken Blue[2] give us their list of sinful tendencies, habits we tend not to call sin. It's a fairly inclusive list: laziness, gluttony, alcoholic overindulgence, greed, unbelief, prayerlessness, unkindness, gossip, materialism, vanity, pride, neglect of spouse and family, wrong ambitions, a host of harmful habits, critical spirits, grumbling spirits, grouchiness, lack of Christian openness, manipulative tendencies, petty deceit, white lies, black lies, spite, con artistry, selfishness, irresponsibility, fantasy lives, sexual sins. They remark:

> We are not merely naive about sin; we are blind to it. And as churches we have become so because we are worldly. . . . And in our blindness we do not see sin around or within our ranks as it really is. . . . We are too naive about human sinfulness, both inside and outside the church. We tend not to see sin that takes place under our noses, and when we see it, we react with shock and dismay. We do not expect to find sin because we do not know our own hearts.[3]

Gordon MacDonald also makes several interesting comments about our efforts to rank sin as serious and nonserious:

> It is a human tendency, however, to want to spotlight certain misbehaviors that seem worse than others. We do this

because they are particularly repugnant to us in our generation or because we perceive that they have greater consequences than others. And when people are exposed or confess guilt in these categories, we refer to them as fallen. But the truth is that we are all fallen people, whether or not we have been guilty of a *major* misbehavior (emphasis mine).[4]

While I would choose the word *sin* for his use of the word *misbehavior*, I believe MacDonald's point is valid.

When we talk about the need for spiritual restoration and revival *it is imperative that we see sin from God's perspective, not just from our own.* If we view sin only from our perspective, we will rationalize and justify our shortcomings as not terribly significant (particularly when we compare our sin to others' sin) and as permissible for a variety of reasons. But if we see sin, any kind of sin, as causing a serious breach in our fellowship with the Father, we will go to any length to seek our restoration with Him. God wants relationship with us. He will do whatever is necessary to restore that relationship. The fact that we don't many times pursue intense relationship with Him is a serious indictment of our spiritual condition.

We must begin every day with this searching inquiry of ourselves, asking God's Holy Spirit to identify sin in our lives. Then we have to deal with that sin, first vertically along the lines set forth in 1 John 1:9, and then horizontally, if that sin has affected others. In the process of identifying sin, all of us will realize our tremendous need for God's forgiveness, mercy, and grace, as well as the significance of verses such as Lamentations 3:22-23: "Because of the Lord's great love we are not consumed, for His compassions never fail. They are new every morning; great is Your faithfulness." Thus we will have cause to celebrate His great love, His compassion, His forgiveness, and His faithfulness.

GUIDELINES TO SPIRITUAL RESTORATION

Previously we have discussed Ezra. As a leader he possessed the critical qualities needed for spiritual restoration or revival. What are these qualities?

1. *Ezra was faithful, obedient, and had a heart devoted first to God, and then to the assigned task.* Somehow

we have a tendency to overlook this quality. After all, we all are committed people to some extent. And we work hard at our devotion to God while trying to be obedient. Many times all of that purposeful devotion stays private and seldom finds corporate expression. While we have discussed at length the appropriateness of and the leader's need for spiritual *inner* qualities, in the context of an organization the ultimate expression of those inner qualities must become visible to the people.

If you are a leader in a Christian organization, whether pastor, president, or executive director, you must become more concerned about your godly character (as God sees and knows you) than about your reputation with your people. Notes Henri Nouwen: "The question is not: how many people take you seriously? How much are you going to accomplish? Can you show some results? But: are you in love with Jesus?"[5]

I am learning anew that the quality of my work will be heavily determined by the godly character of my inner commitments. I must pursue my love for God as my paramount calling. The comments of Ezekiel 22:30 reflect perhaps a pending contemporary tragedy: "I looked for a man among them who would build up the wall and stand before Me in the gap on behalf of the land so I would not have to destroy it, but I found none."

2. *For spiritual renewal or revival to occur, sin has to be acknowledged and dealt with.* Again, here is where we have to be brutally honest with God, with ourselves, and with each other. We see in Ezra 9:1-2 a concern for the sin of leaders.

Certain leaders came forward and expressed concern to Ezra that the previous commands forbidding intermarriage with the neighboring pagan countries had been violated, and that "the leaders and officials have led the way in this unfaithfulness." Once the issue of the leaders' sin was "on the table," how did Ezra deal with it? In Ezra's response we see a *third* step in the process of spiritual restoration.

3. *Ezra involved himself in a response, not of outrage, but of public humility and sorrow before the Lord.* He abased himself before the Lord: "I sat there appalled until

the evening sacrifice" (9:4). His response also involved fasting (10:6). There are several reasons why I believe Ezra's action was appropriate for a leader. I want to suggest only one. As a leader, if I first humble myself before God before I act, quietly reflecting on my own life and character and the nature of a subsequent response, this has a way of guarding my intent and my motive. It assures me of both cleanness of heart (private) and cleanness of action (public). As someone has suggested, all of us must be alert to the reality that many of our assumptions about others are aroused by our knowledge of ourselves.

4. *Next Ezra prayed before the Lord.* "Then, at the evening sacrifice, I arose from my self-abasement, with my tunic and cloak torn, and fell on my knees with my hands spread out to the Lord my God and prayed" (9:5). In his prayer, he included himself as he expressed concern for *"our* sins" and *"our* guilt" (verse 6, emphasis mine). He not only identified with the people, but he allowed for the fact that he too in some way might have sinned before the Lord. Notice too that his prayer was public.

5. *Ezra's acts of humility and prayers motivated the people to action.* This is not a situation where Ezra had to badger the people. Rather, while Ezra was praying, the people who had gathered "wept bitterly" (10:1). They told Ezra that they had been unfaithful to the Lord and would support him in any corrective action he wanted to take: "Let it be done according to the Law. Rise up; this matter is in your hands. We will support you, so take courage and do it" (verses 3-4).

Ezra's actions and the people's response suggest the need for public prayer to seek forgiveness from sin which prevents fellowship with the Lord. His actions also suggest that prayer ought to be offered in a spirit of humility and self-abasement. Ezra's prayer was not a prayer for the pagan world but rather for the fallen people of God.

While many evangelicals can recall public prayers for the pagan lost, probably they have heard fewer prayers for those who are fallen brothers. Fewer still have seen visible evidence from the pulpit that sin is a cause for serious distress and tears. Again, think about it. When was the last time you have seen tears and brokenness in the pulpit over the sin of fellow Christians? Ezra reflected this kind of distress in his public life and it profoundly impacted the people around him. I'm convinced that public and genuine brokenness over sin is a key to spiritual restoration.

6. *The action taken to deal with sin followed a process, involved careful investigation, and was specific.* We see from the text that the specific sin forbidden was intermarriage (9:10-12). The process followed was to be based on the Law (10:3) and was to include careful investigation (10:16). Interestingly, the Scripture has identified processes for dealing with both individual and corporate sin (Matthew 18 and 1 Corinthians 5 respectively), yet not many churches follow these practices. Why? Because many churches feel uncomfortable dealing with sin in a "my rights" oriented society. Dealing with both individual and corporate sin is a critical element of spiritual restoration.

BROKENNESS AND SPIRITUAL RESTORATION

Thus far, we have talked about tears, certain kinds of spiritual activity, and fasting, steps which if genuinely pursued out of a proper motivation to deal with sin and find spiritual restoration, I believe God could respond to by sending revival.

However, we ought not fool ourselves into believing that tears alone or religious activities such as fasting will of themselves automatically produce revival. Examples of these things failing to impress God are found in Isaiah 58:3-6; Hosea 6:6; Joel 2:13; Amos 5:21-23; and Malachi 2:13-16.

Genuine brokenness which produces repentance, however, can be an important part of spiritual restoration and revival. Furthermore, some argue that we ought to see brokenness as a gift. James Houston, in a presentation at Regent College, observed that "we can volunteer for brokenness, and sometimes God gives us the gift of brokenness. And in that brokenness we begin anew." Sometimes we look at our spiritual walk as something we can manipulate for results, including being broken, anytime we choose to do so. We tell ourselves that we'll take care of that "sin" tomorrow. So we pack off God into our little box until we're ready to do Him the favor of doing what He wants us to do. We assume that we can push this button, pull that lever, play this song, and pray that prayer, and presto—people will become broken.

Our sometimes simplistic attitudes and our presumption on God in these matters reminds me of the story of Simon the sorcerer, found in Acts 8. He had been impressing people with his greatness and his magic until the Apostle Philip came onto the scene. Many, including Simon the sorcerer, heard Philip's message, believed, and were baptized. Peter and John later arrived in Samaria to visit these new believers, laying hands on them, and giving them the Holy Spirit. Simon was so impressed with Peter and John that he offered them money if they gave him this gift "so that everyone on whom I lay my hands may receive the Holy Spirit" (verses 18-19). Peter rebuked Simon for thinking that this gift could be bought, saying, "Perhaps He [the Lord] will forgive you for having such a thought in your heart" (verse 22).

Simon's fault, it seems to me, is often our own. Even though the Scripture clearly notes that Simon believed and was baptized (verse 13), he thought that through some effort of his own (here the payment of money) he could receive the Holy Spirit. Peter's response clearly indicates that receiving the Holy Spirit was a gift from God, not something that could be purchased. We too need to look at all that God gives us as a gift. We have to stop attempting to manipulate God for our private benefit. We need to pursue God's forgiveness of our sin as a matter of the highest order.

The Scripture further makes this point in several ways. First, repentance, whether for salvation or for dealing with sin in the life of the believer, is usually presented as a matter of great urgency. If I am at the altar prepared to offer a sacrifice and there remember sin against another, even before I offer the sacrifice, I am to go and seek restoration. The day of salvation is usually presented as "today," "now." We dare not presume on the Holy Spirit in these matters.

Second, the spiritual work that is done in our lives is usually presented as something God does in us rather than as something we do alone. It is His gift to us. I was reminded of this anew after reading the newsletter of our local church in which the pastor made the following helpful observations:

> I have a firm conviction that Christlikeness is not an achievement; it is a GIFT. In the midst of his discourse on Christ's humility in the Epistle to the Philippians (chapter 2), Paul says, "God is at work in you, both to will and to work for His good pleasure." The notion that we may become more ... like Jesus through earnest effort ... puts both the responsibility and achievement of Christlikeness on us. We become Christlike only to the degree in which we are willing to open up every facet of our lives to His lordship and His kingship. It is not our effort nor our energy that makes us like Christ. ... It is God at work IN us both to will and to work for HIS good pleasure.[6]

Certainly, we can open or close ourselves to God's work in our lives through belief or unbelief. To be sure, we can confess our sin. But it is God who grants forgiveness. It is His work, not ours alone. We need to accept what He does for us and in us—whether through tears and brokenness or something else—as His gift to us. We can't buy revival; we can't weep revival into being. We *can* pray for revival but only the Spirit of God can bring revival.

CONCLUSION

We have seen in this chapter that the Lord has an intense desire for His people to be "hot" in their walk with Him. His strong dislike for spiritual indifference is evident in Revelation 3:15: "I know your deeds, that you are neither cold nor hot. I wish you were either one or the other."

We have also looked at the need for personal renewal in leadership. I remain persuaded that a connection exists between personal renewal and my willingness to honor the concept of the Sabbath, whenever celebrated. Further, knowing that we cannot manage or manipulate revival, I am nevertheless convinced that personal renewal, and its results, will make it likelier to see spiritual restoration in my life.

Finally, there seems to be a clear relationship in the Scripture between my "being still" and my "knowing God."

My desire at this point of my life, as a leader in process, is to be still and to know God, increasingly better.

QUESTIONS FOR FURTHER THOUGHT AND DISCUSSION

1. Do you see differences between spiritual restoration and revival? What are they? What are the similarities?
2. Do you see revival as "ongoing" or a "one-time" experience?
3. If your church sponsors "revival services," what is the expected result? How are these services different from other church services? Should they be different?
4. Do you agree that the church has more or less separated sin into "serious" and "nonserious" categories? If so, how and in what way? In your view does the Scripture categorize sin this way?
5. Do people need to be rehabilitated from the scars of all sin or just "serious" sin? In what ways do you tolerate "little" sins?
6. What elements are essential to seeing revival take place in your life? In your church? Where does it begin? When?
7. How do you see brokenness relating to spiritual restoration? Recall that Peter sinned and was restored. Paul murdered and blasphemed and was restored. David murdered and committed adultery but was restored. Moses murdered and was restored. Each was broken by God in some way.
8. Are there not other biblical examples, however, of people like Daniel and Joseph, who maintained consistency in their walk with the Lord? Were they ever broken? Was there a need for them to experience brokenness? What role did hardship and suffering play in keeping their walk with God on the cutting edge?

LEADERS AND THE LOCAL CHURCH

Many Christians who hold both formal and informal positions of leadership in organizations outside the local church see themselves as "just a layperson." They are not meaningfully involved within the church, despite their scriptural responsibility to do so. In his book, *Unleashing the Church*, Frank Tillapaugh observes: "The church's main problem is getting lay people involved in ministry."[1]

Whether or not one agrees with Tillapaugh's assessment, it is probably fair to observe that most churches are not overrun with active lay participation. We need to do better—much better. Indeed, the paradox is that without an active laity, the local church is doomed to struggle, if not failure. Unfortunately, many are content with that state of events, including laypersons and particularly those who lead outside the church. Before we further discuss this issue and what we might do about it, we need to define our terms.

THE CHURCH AND ITS PEOPLE

When I use the term *laity* or *layperson*, I am referring to that individual who does *not* hold a full-time *paid* position in the work of the local church. When I use the term *church*, I am *not* talking about a church building. While a church building may have legal and organizational standing, in the biblical sense a church building is simply one of the locations where the church meets. God doesn't dwell there.

I find of interest those many efforts made by well-intentioned people who suggest that the church building is like the temple of the Old Testament. But I am reminded of Solomon's observation: "But who is able to build a temple for Him, since the heavens, even the highest heavens, cannot contain Him?" (2 Chronicles 2:6)

Recall for a moment Jesus' dialogue with the Samaritan woman (John 4:4-26). She was in essence arguing for a special worship location when she said: "Our fathers worshiped on this mountain, but you Jews claim that the place where we must worship is in Jerusalem" (verse 20). Yet Jesus responded: "A time is coming and *has now come* when the true worshipers will worship the Father in spirit and truth, for they are the kind of worshipers the Father seeks. God is spirit, and His worshipers must worship in spirit and in truth" (verses 23-24, emphasis mine). And Paul, after telling his readers that he had "laid a foundation as an expert builder," reminds them: "Don't you know that you yourselves are God's temple and that God's spirit lives in you?" (1 Corinthians 3:16)

Well, then what is the church? According to Ephesians 1:22-23, "God placed all things under [Christ's] feet and appointed Him to be head over everything for the *church* which is His body, the fullness of Him who fills everything in every way" (emphasis mine). There we have it! Christ's body is the church. But what constitutes His body? Romans 12:4-5 supplies the answer: "Just as each of us has one body with many members, and these members do not all have the same function, so in Christ we who are many form one body, and each member belongs to all the others."

It appears, then, that all of us, leaders *and* followers, are part of the body of Christ if we have invited Him to be the Saviour and Lord of our lives. *We* constitute His body. As Paul writes, "Now you are the body of Christ, and each one of you is a part of it" (1 Corinthians 12:27).

As we study more carefully the biblical teaching on this subject we learn one more very important piece of truth: As part of the body of Christ, *we each play a necessary or vital role.* Some of the functions the body parts perform include teaching, giving, serving, and leading (see

Romans 12:4-8; 1 Corinthians 12:1-18; Ephesians 4:4-16; 1 Peter 4:10-11). In short, the church is composed of persons who have accepted Christ and who are fully prepared to exercise the spiritual gifts God has gifted them with.

Christ's body has no organizational membership requirements for admission or inclusion. We can't find biblical support for a position that says "only members of the legally incorporated XYZ church can participate in our programs and activities." Indeed, persons who hold to this position not only incompletely define the biblical church but replace biblical expectations of the body with a set of manmade requirements for involvement. While there may be good *organizational* reasons to argue for membership in a local church, and I believe there are, we *cannot* equate membership in a local church or denomination with membership in the body of Christ. Parenthetically, might this be one of the reasons a significant number of laypersons are not involved in the work of ministry? While we complain about lack of lay involvement, we tend to shut out their involvement at the same time. Again, we need to return to the biblical standard in this area.

From this brief review, then, I believe it's biblically incorrect to say that the pastor or the pastoral staff should be the *only* ones involved in the work of ministry. While paid staff, to be sure, are to be involved in the work of the church, the work of the church is not to be *only* for paid church staff. Rather, Scripture teaches that each Christian, as a member of the body of Christ, has the responsibility for doing his or her part of the work of the church. And this includes lay persons, those who lead and those who follow.

LAYPEOPLE ARE ESSENTIAL TO THE WORK

First, as we have just noted, without the involvement of laypeople, gifts and abilities needed for the body of Christ to function properly are simply not present. Indeed, there can be no healthy body without having all its parts involved and working properly.

All of us can point to mechanical examples of this principle. What amazes me is that we take such a cavalier attitude about lay noninvolvement in our churches. Lay noninvolvement ought to drive us to our knees. We should make every reasonable effort to encourage participation, whether or not church membership is required. None of us seems to be satisfied with a mechanical malfunction. Why are we content with a spiritual one? If only a few persons are using their gifts, what we end up with is an incomplete body—an exhausted body with only one foot, or one eye, or one arm. I would add that it appears that God has given at least one gift to each believer. If one did not have a gift, how would that person be a necessary part of the body?

Tillapaugh gives a *second* reason why laypeople are essential to the church. As he observes, ministry by lay-people, including lay leaders, "must be taken seriously, since there are so many *more* laypeople and they can do so *much more* ministry."[2] His point is a good one. What pastor has not used the text that the harvest is great but the laborers are few? Ironically, many pastoral staffs unknowingly develop programs which tend to discourage lay involvement except in a very narrow sphere.

There is a *third* reason for lay involvement—an involved active laity, involved with front-line ministry, will be more supportive of the church and its programs than a noninvolved, rear-echelon motivated laity. According to Tillapaugh:

> If we are involved in *front-line* ministries, we will be involved in people's lives. We will be dealing with them over issues such as salvation, repentance, spiritual growth and deepening the level of fellowship with our Lord and other believers . . . whatever the context, the objective of a front-line ministry is always the same—to see one another rooted, built up in Christ. . . . In contrast, *rear-echelon* ministries are concerned primarily with planning and programming. The issues tend to be: How are we going to keep the sidewalks clear? What contractor are we going to use? How are we going to get the water fountain fixed? Which materials are we going to use in the high school Sunday School class? Then there is, of course, the ever present question, who can we get to take the vacant spot on our committee?[3]

WHY ARE MORE LAYPERSONS NOT INVOLVED IN MINISTRY?

First, and surprising to many, is that some *pastors don't want extensive numbers of laypersons involved in ministry*. Surprised? Let me illustrate how this might be the case. For example, many pastors don't take laypersons, including those who lead, very seriously and secondly, simply don't trust laypersons to be involved in ministry. Again, note the words of Tillapaugh:

> I am convinced that many more laypeople will accomplish great tasks when they become convinced that we pastors are *serious* about allowing them to *do* ministry.... Unfortunately, church leaders ... are often not accustomed to trusting people with ministry.... This style of ministry lessens their (pastoral) control.[4]

Many lay leaders, particularly those in leadership positions outside the church, are sometimes viewed as a personal threat to the pastor. Yet as Willimon and Wilson note, "The clergy must trust the layperson to witness to [his] experience of the grace of God, not simply to serve on the finance committee.... We need to trust the laypeople to have the best interests of their church at heart."[5]

Pastors discourage participation another way—by *creating a sense of distance* between how much the pastor knows (and how well equipped) and how little the layperson knows (and how poorly equipped). It's a kind of spiritualized "we're better than you." Again, note the words of Willimon and Wilson: "Too many of our clergy feel that laypeople do not really understand the Christian faith, even though it is the laity who give meaning and purpose to the pastoral ministry in the first place."[6] Yet they remind us that, "the clergy themselves are all *secondary* inventions of the church."[7]

They give us an extensive case study of John Wesley and his ministry in England to illustrate their concerns. "The Wesleyan revival in 18th century England was in great part John Wesley's inspired attempt to reform the established Church of England through a reformation of the laity.... Wesley knew enough ... to know the laity are the church.... He sought to use his lay preachers as a means

of reinstating the parishes of the Church of England...."
While Wesley was classically educated at Oxford, "his true
genius lay in his ability to speak to the laypeople in ways
that could be understood and appropriated in everyday
life." His argument for extensive use of the laity in ministry
"was the Protestant doctrine of the 'priesthood of believers'—the belief that each Christian is . . . to be a priest to
his or her own neighbor." First Peter 2:9-10 addresses the
whole church, not just the clergy when it states: "But you
are a chosen people, a royal priesthood, a holy nation, a
people belonging to God, that you may declare the praises
of Him who called you out of darkness into His wonderful
light. Once you were not a people, but now you are the
people of God; once you had not received mercy, but now
you have received mercy."

As Willimon and Wilson observe, however, before
long, Wesley's church, the Methodist church, "had no room
for lay guidance and input beyond the local church
level." As to the way these differences continue, again,
Willimon and Wilson note the following: "While the pressure to increase the educational requirements for clergy
has many desirable consequences, it is also a means of our
clergy's assuring themselves that the ministry is a 'profession'; similar to medicine or law. . . ." This elevated position
or status is but another subtle way of saying to the
layperson: we'll let you be involved in selected areas of
ministry, but only after we're sure you're qualified to do
so." Ironically, Willimon and Wilson observe that it is
usually the clergy, *not the laity*, which exerts pressure for
increased educational requirements for ordination: "The
gap between laity and clergy has widened with increased
educational requirements for ordination. It should be
noted that the pressure to increase the educational requirements of clergy has come from the ministers, not the
laity."[8]

In this way, we must be careful of how laypersons
might perceive the pastorate in our own churches and, in
turn, be discouraged from lay ministry because of their
perceived inadequacy or lack of knowledge.

What are some of the ways laypersons can be encouraged to participate in the ministry of the church?

PASTORAL EFFORTS WHICH CAN ENCOURAGE LAY INVOLVEMENT

First, the senior pastor of the church must be willing to release laypeople for ministry. Observes Tillapaugh:

> If he (the senior pastor) chooses not to share the leadership of the ministry in any significant way, he is responsible for that choice. . . . If the senior pastor is not willing to actually share the ministry, *the church unleashed will remain a dream.*"

And then Tillapaugh makes the following observation: "There is something woefully stifling to the ministry of the church when its people constantly get the message, 'I am the pastor.' "[10]

Second, the pastoral staff must use terms which encourage lay involvement. For example, I am surprised at the many pastors who refer to themselves as *the* minister. My suggestion would be for them to refer to themselves as pastors or pastor-teachers. I well remember one church I attended where this label was applied, followed with these words in the bulletin: "Every member, a minister." I have seen that expanded to "every person, a ministry." While the pastoral staff does minister, so too should *all* church members and attenders (who are Christians).

With regard to this second example, I would suggest great care to avoid referring to the church as a building. Phrases such as "Be quiet, this is God's house" or "Come to our church" misrepresent and confuse scriptural truth. If as laypersons we fail to understand just what the church is, we will surely fail to carry out the ministry of the church.

Third, the pastoral staff must present to laypeople not only the vision of the church gathered but also the vision of the church scattered. Again, I see this emphasis as particularly important for those laypersons who hold leadership assignments outside the church. When I use the term *the church gathered* I'm referring to those occasions when the members of the body of Christ come together as a group, large or small, for worship, admonition, rebuke, and exhortation—to name but a few of the church's purposes. I have in mind a verse like Hebrews 10:24-25: "And let us consider how we may spur one another on toward love and good deeds. Let us not give up meeting together, as some are in the habit of doing, but let us encourage one another—and all the more as you see the Day approaching."

When I use the term *the church scattered* I have in mind the various "members" (I use this term loosely) going "into all the world" to do ministry, whether as leaders or followers, so that the world may see Christ and give glory to the Father in heaven (Matthew 5:16). On the other hand, it is difficult for some to think of lay responsibility beyond a church gathered. For example, in reflecting on one of their interviews with a given pastor, Robert Bellah and his coauthors of *Habits of the Heart* made this observation: "He (the pastor) was perhaps too quick to assume that Christian commitment meant taking some organizational or committee responsibility within the parish."[11]

Let me illustrate this further. If, as a layman, I think of ministry only as the church *gathered*, I soon observe that there are only a *finite* number of jobs needing to be done when the church is gathered. There are only so many choir slots, Sunday School teacher slots, board slots. When these positions are filled, they're filled. The larger the church gathered, the more acute the problem with the layperson saying, "There's no place for me to exercise my gift."

However, when we think of the church *scattered*, an *infinite* number of opportunities exist for lay service and ministry. There are literally hundreds of thousands of circles, or what the Navigators call "spheres of influence," which laypersons regularly frequent and where pastoral staff would find entry extremely difficult. We must both encourage and release laypersons for ministry in this context.

This leads logically to a *fourth* observation: The pastoral staff needs to think about *diversified ministry*—broadly defined, managed, and operated by laypersons—rather than to think of ministry in only the more narrow or traditional church-gathered ways.

Tillapaugh observes that pastoral staffs tend to have a limited, sometimes "traditional" view of ministry. As such, ministry opportunities for laypersons tend to be limited:

We tend to think everyone ought to be like us. If a formal worship service where everyone wears a coat and tie is best for me, I'm likely to think that it's best for everyone. If a marriage encounter weekend revolutionized my marriage, it will revolutionize everyone's marriage. If I find the "key" to my spiritual life is a witnessing seminar, everybody will find the key there. We try to fit everyone into our experiences. But God simply doesn't work that way. People need the *diversity* within the body to find what is best for them, not necessarily wnat we're sure they need.[12]

Tillapaugh goes on to explain how his church works at this diversification of the church gathered:

If people don't like my preaching, they can go to Pastor Thompson's congregation. If they enjoy a formal service with a choir, fine, it's available. If not, there are informal services. If they like to wear jeans to church and want to bring friends who live in jeans, they can choose a service that is compatible. If they feel we ought to be engaged in doing a certain ministry, we're willing to listen and work with them.[13]

In large part, a number of *church-gathered programs* are more the products of a church culture than of a reflection of New Testament practice, let alone biblical mandates. One would be hard-pressed to find a Sunday morning worship/Sunday School/Sunday evening/Wednesday night prayer meeting schedule supported by either New Testament practice or teaching. Yet these practices continue to move forward in our organized churches seemingly unchallenged because that's the way it's always been. My sense is that many pastors would be delighted to experiment with changes in these schedules but can't because of concern from the laity. I must confess that I struggled a bit upon hearing that, because of space problems, a church with which I am familiar has gone to a Saturday night *and* two Sunday morning services. But why not? This represents the kind of flexibility and diversity I have in mind.

Again, we must be open to *diversity* both to the ministries of the church gathered and the ministries of the church scattered.

Fifth, we ought to be involving laypersons more extensively in the services and programs of the church gathered. One of my joys as I visit a variety of churches is to see the ways laypeople are involved—from reading the

Scripture and making announcements to introducing new members they personally sponsored.

I would argue that, at a minimum, the pastoral staff ought to take responsibility for the preaching assignment but, beyond that, I think much of the remaining service could be directed by trained laypersons. Interestingly, many laypersons (and pastors) want the pastor to be in the limelight in scheduled services because that's their expectation of what pastors do (and the way laypeople have been trained to think). Having laypersons so involved would be an excellent statement to other laypersons in the church that lay ministry is crucial and necessary. Tragically, many churches limit Sunday morning lay involvement to ushering, collecting the offering, or musical participation.

CONCLUSION

Given the church's mandate, it is imperative that lay leaders—indeed, all laypersons—become more actively involved in the local church. For those who hold leadership positions in organizations outside the church, this ought *not* be used as an excuse for noninvolvement in the local church.

It's also time for the church to unleash its laity. And it is time for the pastoral staff to say, "We, both laypersons and pastoral staff, are the church. And as the pastoral staff, we're here to serve, enable, and equip you, as laypersons. As shepherds of the flock, we will lead you not by 'driving' but by 'helping.'" And as the biblical shepherd, the pastor-shepherd will not be satisfied with having only 75 of 100 sheep following and in the fold. Rather, the pastor-shepherd works and labors, giving his life if necessary, until not just 99 but *all* are in the fold.

It's time for laypersons and for those of us involved in vocational Christian leadership outside the church to admit that it is also our fault if the church is not flourishing. As we have noted, the mission of the church will *not* be accomplished unless all parts of the body are involved and fully exercising their gifts. Vocational Christian ministry outside the local church ought not be a substitute for involvement within the local church.

While persons like Ezra, Isaiah, Aaron, Samuel, and

143

other priest-and-pastor types played key roles in the work of God, so too did leaders such as Joseph, Moses, Daniel, David, Solomon, Paul (the tentmaker), Luke, Joshua, and Gideon. This latter group was all laymen (some bi-vocational), leaders and followers.

It's time to quit talking about which group, the pastoral staff or the laity, is most important. The church needs both. The work, ministry, and dreams of the church will not happen effectively without an unleashed laity and an unselfish leadership, each enabled and empowered by the Holy Spirit to do His ministry.

*   *   *   *   *

In the final three chapters of the book we will study in greater depth some of the leaders in the Bible. How did their lives reflect the roles of leading and following? How did they cultivate their walk by faith and at the same time lead? Were they always "perfect" leaders? While we'll look at some New Testament characters, we'll spend most of our time looking at Old Testament characters. A major reason for this is that in the Old Testament, we tend to see a more complete picture of leaders in action in a variety of roles.

QUESTIONS FOR FURTHER THOUGHT AND DISCUSSION

1. As a lay leader in the local church, do you know your spiritual gift? How do you know this? How do you know it is not just one of your interests?
2. As a general question, would you say the great majority of the laypeople in your local church know with certainty their spiritual gift?
3. Are you involved in the local church exercising and using your spiritual gift(s)? As the terms have been used in this chapter, are you involved in "front-line" or "rear-echelon" ministry?
4. Are laypersons in your church seriously sought out by the pastoral staff to do lay ministry? In what kinds of lay ministry are laypersons involved—other than as ushers, choir members, or Sunday School teachers? Should they be? Why or why not?

5. In what kinds of "church scattered" ministries are laypersons in your church involved?

6. If you could begin any "ministry" associated with your local church over the next six months, whether church-gathered or church-scattered, what would it be?

7. If you are a pastor-teacher, as I have used the term, how do you direct your ministry extensively toward laypersons and still enlist significant and necessary political support? If a layperson, what counsel do you give your pastor on this matter?

8. Given the parables of Jesus in Luke 15 (these ought to be read and studied before proceeding further), do they speak in any way to the issue of whether or not there should be threshold levels of congregational support in order to justify pastoral continuance or departure? How should such support be ascertained? How often? Is it practical to insist on or to expect 100 percent support? Do these parables apply only to salvation?

CHAPTER
TEN

ABEL, NOAH, AND JOB

ABEL

Abel is probably one of the least studied characters in the Bible, at least from a leadership perspective. What do we know about him? From Genesis 4, we learn that his parents were Adam and Eve. He had an older brother, Cain. Cain worked the soil and grew crops and Abel was a shepherd, taking care of flocks. At some time (the Scripture states "in the course of time"), presumably beyond childhood, Cain and Abel brought offerings to the Lord. Cain brought "fruits of the soil" (verse 3) and Abel brought "fat portions from some of the firstborn of his flock" (verse 4).

The Lord looked with favor on Abel and his offering but with disfavor on Cain and his offering. The text doesn't tell us that God had previously given them instructions on what kind of offering to bring. The text also doesn't tell us that the reason for God's disfavor with Cain was because he brought something from the ground while Abel brought something from his flock. Perhaps Abel brought his offering in a spirit which was more pleasing to God. God's favoritism made Cain angry. Cain was given an opportunity by the Lord "to do what was right" so that he too could enjoy God's favor. Cain refused and instead set out on a plan whereby he subsequently killed his brother Abel. Thereafter he suffered an ongoing curse and punishment from the Lord.

Interestingly, even though we don't know much about

Abel from the Genesis account, our Lord commends him twice for his righteousness (Matthew 23:35; Luke 11:51) as does John (1 John 3:12). In Hebrews 11:4 and 12:24 we find additional insight about Abel, which helps us understand reasons why he was commended for his righteousness. What are they and what can we learn about Abel which might be useful in our quest to be better leaders and followers?

First, *Abel was sensitive to God's presence in his life.* Genesis 4 suggests that one of Cain's biggest concerns about his punishment from God was that he would no longer be able to experience God's presence: "Today You are driving me from the land, and ⸀ will be hidden from Your presence" (verse 14). Abel, unlike Cain, apparently made special efforts to be in the presence of God. Perhaps this is why Abel chose the kind of offering he brought, or perhaps why he came to God with the right attitude.

Second, *Abel's sensitivity to God kept his heart pure.* Abel obviously came to the place of sacrifice with a pure heart; that is why elsewhere in Scripture Abel is always called righteous. Presumably Cain could have chosen to change his attitude and/or his offering (verses 6-7) so that he also could experience God's favor, but he opted otherwise.

Third, because he was sensitive to God's presence and to keeping his heart pure, *Abel was able to make his offering to God an act of faith and obedience.* The writer of Hebrews says it this way: "By faith Abel offered God a better sacrifice than Cain did" (11:4).

Being sensitive to God's presence, keeping my heart pure, and reflecting obedience to Him and to His commands are all essentials of being a Christian leader. There are times in leadership when taking a particular action just doesn't make sense from a human perspective. Yet if we are confident that the action in question is of the Lord, we take it anyway.

There is yet a fourth observation we need to make about Abel: *Because of his willingness to practice faithful obedience to God's direction, Abel lost his life.* Obedient followership many times exacts a high price, sometimes even death. Abel was killed by his brother Cain, who acted in jealous rage. Why? Because the disobedient Cain had convinced himself that "God liked Abel best" while all along God had communicated to Cain a different reason for His disfavor.

Depending in which society and country one practices leading and following, death may result. But even when it does not, the leader may suffer other "hardships." Faithful followers of God through the ages have been willing to incur hardship in order to remain faithful. So it continues. Their willingness to pay the cost illustrates their commitment to this inner side of leading and following.

NOAH

The Prophet Ezekiel discusses with great fervor God's disappointment with His chosen people and His impending judgment. Things have gotten so bad, announces Ezekiel, that "even if these three men—Noah, Daniel, and Job— were in it, they could only save themselves by their righteousness, declares the Sovereign Lord" (Ezekiel 14:14). What was it about these three leaders that makes them examples of righteousness? Here we'll look only at Noah and Job. Later we'll also look at Daniel.

The primary texts which detail Noah's life are found in Genesis 5–9. While we don't know much about his vocation in life we do know that, like Cain, Noah was a man of the soil, a farmer: "Noah, a man of the soil, proceeded to plant a vineyard" (9:20). It is likely that Noah had practiced farming before he was called to build the ark and perhaps continued with his farming while the ark was being built. We also know that Noah was a "preacher of righteousness" (2 Peter 2:5). We're not told whether or not he was a man of wealth, but he obviously had access to material resources given the costs and material needed to build the ark.

God certainly was impressed with Noah's righteousness:

But Noah found favor in the eyes of the Lord (Genesis 6:8).

Noah was a righteous man, blameless among the people of his time, and he walked with God (6:9).

I have found you righteous in this generation (7:1).

148

Whatever other qualities Noah may have possessed, righteousness with God was an important one that qualified him for a position of leadership. Note the similarity between God's description of Noah and Paul's observations about spiritual leaders in 1 Timothy 3 which we previously discussed.

I have not read many books that have identified Noah as a leader, a person to be emulated and compared with the likes of Moses, David, and Joshua. Just what did Noah do and how did he exercise leadership?

Like many other Bible leaders, God called Noah to a specific task. We don't know whether or not Noah was given a choice to refuse. Given God's intentions and the tragic personal results which would have taken place had Noah not been obedient, Noah obeyed. Perhaps those who are in tune with God are always the ones prepared to carry out His bidding. Perhaps it is no coincidence that those who are qualitatively prepared to lead, despite their own doubts, are the ones asked to lead. Sometimes God needs to prod a bit as He did with Gideon and Moses.

What was the task that God called Noah to? At first glance it would appear that he was called to be the builder of a large ship. Upon further reflection, however, Noah's provision of a large ship was simply the means to carry out the assigned task—the preservation of the human race and animalkind. God, of course, had purposed to destroy major parts of His created world because of "man's wickedness on the earth. . . . The Lord was grieved that He had made man on the earth" (6:5-6).

Other than the task of our Lord of reconciling the world to Himself, and the task He has given us of sharing the good news with others, probably no more important leadership assignment has been given than what God gave Noah. When we think of our various corporate responsibilities, few are of greater magnitude.

Over a period of many years Noah finally completed the ark. While to build a boat this large was a major task, trying to comprehend a flood was perhaps an even more difficult assignment, given the fact that Noah and the people of his time had probably not yet experienced large amounts of rain. While the physical assignment was considerable, there was also a "faith" assignment, that of taking God at His word.

The Flood eventually came, the ark and its contents were preserved, and as was the case of Adam and Eve before them, Noah and his sons were commanded to "be fruitful and increase in number and fill the earth" (9:1). God then established a new covenant with Noah and his sons: "I now establish My covenant with you and with your descendants after you" (verse 9). What can we learn from Noah to help us better understand leading and following? Let me suggest several lessons:

1. *Noah was available and qualified for his leadership assignment before it was made known to him.* Too often, in our efforts to develop and train leaders, the focus of our efforts is on some actual future leadership assignment that is often aspired to. We don't see this kind of ambition from Noah. He was content in his livelihood and was not seeking some new challenge to conquer. Yet all along he was developing the kinds of qualities that would ultimately qualify him for his important leadership assignment. One of the things this says to me is that regardless of whether or not I will ever be involved with a formal leadership role, I need to be building into my life the qualities that will enhance such an assignment. And for the Christian leader godliness of life is an essential prerequisite.

As we'll see elsewhere, I am continually amazed as to how the God of the Old Testament and the Christ of the New Testament went about selecting leaders. Often the person selected was in some obscure, insignificant position—shepherd, tax collector, fisherman, soldier. Sometimes there appears to be a bit of randomness to the process. Yet the possession of the proper inner qualities, often imperfectly reflected, coupled with a growing willingness to depend on the Father, seemed to be enough.

2. *Noah completed what he was asked to do.* I am impressed with the completeness of Noah's obedience, even when the task seemingly made no sense. What if Noah had delayed in the task? What if he negotiated for a smaller ark? What if he had insisted on answers to all his questions before he began, questions such as, how will the animals, reptiles, and birds find their way here? What is a

flood? And there were no doubt "why" questions that could have cost precious time. Why this judgment? Why this method of judgment and deliverance? Why only us? Simply put, Noah carried out the assigned task, completely.

Often God's methods or means of deliverance don't make sense from a purely human perspective. Given our tendencies toward pragmatism and our desire for actions that are rational, we often struggle with a God who says only "obey and follow." Perhaps, like us, Noah wanted more information, more reasons that made "human" sense. But the fact that he did not get them did not deter him from the assigned task.

Noah carried out the assigned task completely even when it required incredible faith and incredible action. I see myself many times running or tempted to run from tough assignments (remember Jonah?). Maybe I cleverly disguise my flight as "a better job" or a "better professional opportunity." That in fact may be the case but I must assure myself that I'm not running. Many times it is easier to run from position to position than it is to stay put and complete a tough assignment. Sometimes staying is more difficult than leaving. Noah stayed with the task and completed it.

3. *Noah preserved his testimony for God in the midst of incredible sin.* In fact, the text tells us God was so grieved by man's sin that He intended to destroy His previous creation. Yet here was Noah, faithful in his service to the Lord in the middle of all of this sin, and in fact condemning the world. Interestingly, Noah did all of this by faith: "By faith Noah, when warned about things not yet seen, in holy fear built an ark to save his family. By his faith he condemned the world and became heir of the righteousness that comes by faith" (Hebrews 11:7).

Leaders and followers are called upon by God to maintain their Christian testimony in the midst of a secular, watching world, often hostile to the things of God. This is tough to do apart from God's grace and the Holy Spirit's leadership. But persist we must if we, like Noah, are to faithfully follow our Lord. We have much to learn from Noah, the leader.

JOB

While Job is often studied and commended for his approach to suffering in his life, we seldom discuss him in the context of leadership. Yet here was a person who had learned to follow and lead.

In today's culture, Job surely would have been on the list of the "Fortune 500." His possessions were many and his influence vast. Indeed, Job "was the greatest man among the people of the East" (Job 1:3). Despite Job's business empire, his family remained a priority to him. They regularly got together for "good times" and Job just as regularly prayed for them. Job also maintained his all-important relationship with his Heavenly Father: "This man was blameless and upright; he feared God and shunned evil" (verse 1).

Unknown to Job, he was about to become the object of a heavenly contest. Satan was convinced that the only reason Job was faithful to the Lord was because of the material blessings God had given Job. God demurred and gave Satan permission to take away all that Job possessed: "Very well, then, everything he has is in your hands, but on the man himself do not lay a finger" (verse 12).

In due course and over a very short period of time, Job proceeded to lose all of his possessions, and, with the exception of his wife, all of his family as well. Job's reaction to all of this? "Then he fell to the ground in worship and said, 'Naked I came from my mother's womb, and naked I will depart. The Lord gave and the Lord has taken away; may the name of the Lord be praised.' In all of this, Job did not sin by charging God with wrongdoing" (verses 20-22).

Satan was still not satisfied. The text in fact suggests that God once again brought Job to Satan's attention: "Have you considered my servant Job? There is no one on earth like him; he is blameless and upright, a man who fears God and shuns evil. And he still maintains his integrity, though you incited Me against him to ruin him without reason" (2:3). Satan countered that if Job's body were subjected to much suffering, then Job would ultimately curse God. God's response? "Very well, then, he is in your hands; but you must spare his life" (verse 6).

Thus begins Satan's second attack against Job, in which he inflicted Job "with painful sores from the soles of his feet to the top of his head" (verse 7). Job's wife counseled her husband to curse God and die. Job's incredible response was that we need to accept trouble from God just as we accept good from Him. Again, Job "did not sin in what he did" (verse 10).

Over the next thirty-five or so chapters, the text records the dialogue between Job and his three friends, Eliphaz, Bildad, and Zophar. Each in his own way attempted to give Job reasons for his setbacks. Job attempted to give his own explanation about his circumstances, making assumptions about God, and posing tough questions to God in the process.

God at last responded to Job, raising all kinds of unanswerable questions of him, each demonstrating in some way His unfathomable greatness. Job was duly humbled and once more acknowledged God's sovereignty. Subsequently, God blessed Job more than He had before, giving him twice the material possessions. And God gave Job another seven sons and three daughters.

What can we learn from Job about leading and following?

1. *Job understood that all of his possessions, all that he had, came from God and belonged to Him.* One thing which gets leaders in trouble is their quest for more possessions. It's not unusual to read newspaper accounts of people quitting one leadership assignment for another because of poor pay. Job's attitude, reflected elsewhere in Scripture, is that we should be content in our circumstances. Note these references:

> Yours, O Lord, is the greatness and the power and the glory and the majesty and the splendor, for everything in heaven and earth is Yours. Yours, O Lord, is the kingdom; You are exalted as head over all. Wealth and honor come from You; You are the ruler of all things. In Your hands are strength and power to exalt and give strength to all (1 Chronicles 29:11-12).

> But godliness with contentment is great gain. For we brought nothing into the world, and we can take nothing out of it (1 Timothy 6:6-7).

Job understood all of this as well. Accordingly, he didn't react negatively when God merely took back what already belonged to Him. This same attitude, when practiced by leaders, transforms attitudes regarding possessions. It's not that a leader shouldn't pursue more goods and a higher salary. But that ought not be one's motivation in leading, and it certainly is no cause for using unbiblical ends to acquire them. Job's understanding about possessions prepared him for his response to their loss.

2. *Job persisted in his love for God and his pursuit of godliness in spite of incredible adversity.* This statement is easy to make but difficult to practice. I have seen people lose family members. I have seen people lose their businesses. I have seen people experience great personal suffering and pain. Job experienced all three. Yet through it all, Job's attitude was: "Shall we accept good from God, and not trouble?" (Job 2:10) Someone has wisely stated, "It doesn't matter where we're going as long as we know who we're following." Job knew *who* he was following. Surely, his response made a positive impression on business colleagues; surely his servants had a better understanding of Job's God because of his response to adversity.

We don't know from this text whether or not Job grieved over the loss of his family and his possessions. In all probability he did. Certainly other Scriptures, including John 11:35 ("Jesus wept") indicate grief is appropriate at the loss of a loved one. We don't know how Job reacted to his other losses, though he did observe that his overall experience of suffering shattered his plans and his heart's desires (Job 17:11). As we'll see shortly, he asked many questions of God. But as a faithful follower of God, Job's perspective was shaped by his knowledge of that God. And that made following easier. What an incredible example to those who lead and follow.

3. *Job was not afraid to ask God hard questions in his attempt to understand what was happening to him.* People who experience adversity often question God, asking difficult things like, "Why was I born in the first place?" (see 3:16; 10:18-19), and "What is man that You make so much of him, that You give him so much attention, that You examine him every morning and test him every moment?" (7:17-18) But in all of his questioning, Job did not query God's sovereignty over his life. Note such verses as:

His wisdom is profound, His power is vast. Who has resisted Him and come out unscathed? (9:4)

If He snatches away, who can stop Him? Who can say to Him, "What are You doing?" (9:12)

To God belong wisdom and power; counsel and understanding are His. What He tears down cannot be rebuilt; the man He imprisons cannot be released (12:13-14).

I still don't have good answers as to why my father passed away at a fairly young age. Yet I accept God's seeming silence on the matter. I appreciate more and more the words of the Apostle Paul in Romans 11:33: "Oh, the depth of the riches of the wisdom and knowledge of God! How unsearchable His judgments and His paths beyond tracing out!"

In a leadership context we often don't know why events happen the way they do. Our task, like that of Job, is to continue to maintain a confidence (not a sense of false bravado) based in the belief expressed so eloquently by the Psalmist David: "By this I will know that *God is for me*" (Psalm 56:9, emphasis mine). Job was so confident in God that he said, "Though He slay me, yet will I hope in Him" (Job 13:15). This was Job's way of saying that his confidence was in the Lord, period. Among other things this statement illustrates God's confidence in Job in the first place. Contrary to what Satan thought, Job loved God for who He was, not for what God could do for him. Job didn't love God only because of the wages God paid him. No health, wealth, and prosperity philosophy here.

4. *Job's attitude in suffering indicated that he was open to learning from this experience.* Reading Job's responses to his questioners as well as Job's own questions, we see his openness to learn more. To his friends he said, "Teach me, and I will be quiet; show me where I have been wrong" (6:24-25). His teachable spirit, that is, his willingness to learn of and from God, is illustrated in Job 9:3: "Though one wished to dispute with Him, he could not answer Him one time out of a thousand." Finally, his response to having been taught new things by God is found in Job 42:2-6:

I know that You can do all things; no plan of Yours can be thwarted. You asked, "Who is this that obscures My counsel without knowledge?" Surely I spoke of things I did not understand, things too wonderful for me to know. You said, "Listen now, and I will speak; I will question you, and you shall answer Me." My ears had heard of You but now my eyes have seen You. Therefore I despise myself and repent in dust and ashes.

Job's continued wonderment of God comes *before* God restored his health, his family, and his other possessions.

One of the qualities for leading and following we have previously seen is a willingness to continue learning. As a result of what Job experienced, he learned anew about God. Perhaps Job wouldn't have learned as much about God or from Him without having experienced the hardships he did. Sometimes hardship prepares people for learning from the Lord in ways that few other things do. As followers who lead and as leaders who follow, we need to be superb learners as God provides, many times, His classroom of hardship education.

5. *Job understood that friends don't always stick closer than a brother at times of adversity.* Job expresses many frustrations during his ordeal. And one that appears to be particularly bothersome to him is the loss of the devotion of trusted friends. His three friends certainly are to be commended for their desire to encourage and comfort Job early in his suffering. Job looked so bad to his friends that they wept over him, tore their robes, and put ashes on their heads. Because they could see how intensely Job was suffering, they stayed with him for seven full days without saying anything (2:11-13).

But when they at last spoke, their words hurt more than they helped. Job complains, "A despairing man should have the devotion of his friends. . . . But my brothers are as undependable as intermittent streams" (6:14-15). Job tells them they are so unfriendly that they "would even cast lots for the fatherless and barter away [their] friend" (6:27). Pretty strong words from Job. We see similar words from David in Psalm 35.

Neither was God pleased with Job's friends. The Lord told one of them, "I am angry with you and your two friends, because you have not spoken of Me what is right, as Job has" (Job 42:7). Accordingly, God told them they had to offer a burnt offering for themselves *and* they needed Job to pray for them. They wisely obeyed and Job offered a prayer on behalf of his three friends, which God accepted.

I really like Job's willingness to continue his friendship with his three friends even after he had been offended by what they had said and even though they apparently were of not much help during his crisis. Interestingly, not until *after* Job had prayed for his friends was he again made prosperous by God.

Somehow in leading and following we have to take this idea of "close friends" much more seriously. As I noted in my previous book, many people have high expectations for the leader. And leaders are not supposed to have friends inside the organization they lead, otherwise the charge of "favoritism" is often leveled. Many times the observation is appropriate. Leaders are also expected not to make themselves vulnerable because, "Who wants to follow a person who has those kinds of problems?"

I want to argue for close friends for both the leader and follower. Whether inside or outside the organization, friends, close friends, are an indispensable part of personhood. How will people be able to bear my burdens if no one else knows about them? My observation is that we probably will never have more than a few close friends and one's best friend, if married, ought to be one's spouse.

Even though Job's friends were not the source of comfort Job needed during his illness, Job nevertheless was willing to pray for them at the end of his illness. Even though they in a way had abandoned him in adversity, Job chose not to abandon them. Keep your friends. They are gifts from God.

CONCLUSION

Abel, Noah, and Job have much to teach us about leading and following. Their faith during times of adversity, their persistence during times of trouble, and their constant confidence in an unfailing Father serve to encourage us all.

QUESTIONS FOR FURTHER THOUGHT AND DISCUSSION

1. How did Abel know the heart of God so that he could please Him with his offering? How is knowing the heart of God important for leading? What reasons produced Cain's disobedience?

2. Why do you think Noah took so long to build the ark? Was it because of its size? Perhaps some disbelief? Limited help? Might God have sent the Flood earlier if the task had been completed earlier? What might this say about God's sense of timing and our efforts in leadership?

3. Do you get the sense that Noah used a lot of people in his building task? Were they primarily family members? What does (or does not) this teach us about delegation and the kind of people we invite to join in a task? Should only Christians be used?

4. Do we get any hint from the Scriptures that Noah was perceived by others as a leader? Do you see Noah as a leader? Why or why not? Must others see and recognize your leadership before you are a leader?

5. How had the Lord been preparing Noah for leadership? What qualities did the Lord think were important for leadership?

6. What were the keys to Noah's surviving the "press of sin and evil" that surrounded his efforts? Might these still be used today?

7. Do you believe that Satan still "presents himself before the Lord" to test leaders as he did Job? What is your evidence for this? Is this what Jesus had in mind in Luke 22:32? Will He always restore things destroyed or people removed (as He did with Job) if we go through something similar?

8. Do you think it's "fair" that God permits this kind of spiritual battle?

9. Do you think Job ever knew that he was the victim of satanic testing? Would he have seen himself as a "victim"? Is personal tragedy in life always the result of this kind of testing? If not, how do you explain it? Does God still test people in the same way?

10. Given what Jesus taught about sin as action, sin as evil thoughts, and sin as the omission of doing good, does Job ever come across sounding somewhat self-righteous? Why or why not?

JOSEPH AND DANIEL

One of the most difficult of the many leadership arenas is "politics." When satisfying the desires of the constituents is often critical to reelection, and when those desires often conflict with the clear teaching of Scripture, it can be difficult to carry out a leadership responsibility.

One former member of the U.S. Congress told me that the only way to survive in Washington and keep your Christian faith intact is to assume that you will not be elected to a subsequent term. Otherwise, the temptation would exist to direct all political action toward getting reelected rather than doing what is best for the constituency and the country. Quite often, biblical obedience and political expediency are mutually incompatible goals.

Jesus was once asked to comment on the potential conflict between being both a citizen of the heavenly kingdom and an earthly one. The issue at question was paying taxes, one which is likewise of no small consequence for contemporary Christians: "Is it right for us to pay taxes to Caesar or not?" (Luke 20:22)

Jesus knew that the people's question was dishonest— He saw "through their duplicity" (verse 23). Indeed, the question was a trap to get the Lord to say something "anti-government," thereby providing His accusers with evidence to discredit Him. So Jesus asked them to bring Him a coin. "Whose portrait and inscription are on it?" "Caesar's," they replied. He said to them, "Then give to Caesar what is

159

Caesar's, and to God what is God's" (verses 24-25). No easy answers here. Jesus' response put the burden clearly back on the inquirers. They would have to sort out what belonged to Caesar and what belonged to God, sometimes no small task.

Whenever we look at biblical examples of leadership, skeptics complain that highlighting those who performed in a theocracy misses the mark, for the most part because our contemporary world is so different. In a theocracy, the religious world and the political world were substantially the same. Accordingly, people like David or Moses weren't always required to wrestle with the "God versus Caesar" questions that Jesus identified.

The two men we will look at in this chapter, Joseph and Daniel, each held significant positions of leadership in a secular government, not a theocracy. As we study their lives and the ways they served God, we'll see how they worked out this "God versus Caesar" dilemma and learn important insights about leading and following.

We'll start with Joseph because he appears in history about 1,000 years or so before Daniel.

JOSEPH'S FAMILY

I want to take several paragraphs to explain Joseph's family background because it provides the context, and some might say pretext, for his involuntary trip to Egypt. Joseph's father was a rich businessman named Jacob (ultimately renamed Israel) and his mother's name was Rachel. Jacob was one of the twin sons of Isaac and Rebekah; his brother was Esau. Joseph probably had heard how his father Jacob had tricked his grandfather Isaac into giving Jacob the birthright that rightfully belonged to Esau.

That tense family relationship is why Jacob had to run away from home to his Uncle Laban's house. Jacob worked many years for Laban in order to marry Laban's daughter and Joseph's mother Rachel, only to be denied her and given Leah instead. The tension between Jacob and Laban eventually caused Jacob to leave and strike out on his own.

While Jacob was still living with Uncle Laban, most of Joseph's half brothers were born. Leah, his mother Rachel's older sister and his father's other wife, had four children—Reuben, Simeon, Levi, and Judah—before Rachel finally accosted Jacob, saying, "Give me children, or I'll die!" (Genesis 30:1) Rachel wanted children so desperately that she gave her husband her servant Bilhah to sleep with. Bilhah had a son, which Rachel named Dan. Bilhah slept with Jacob again, and Rachel named Bilhah's second son Naphtali.

Leah realized that she was temporarily unable to bear children. And seeing Rachel's practice of giving her servant to Jacob, Leah followed suit, giving Jacob her servant Zilpah to sleep with. Zilpah bore two sons, Gad and Asher. Then Leah insisted that Jacob sleep with her on a given night (verse 16) and she conceived and bore Jacob her fifth son, Issachar. Leah followed with a sixth son, Zebulun. (She was also the mother of Dinah.) Still, Rachel had had no children of her own. Finally, she became pregnant and Joseph was born (verses 22-24). He was the last child born while his father was working for Laban. Joseph's only full brother, Benjamin, was born years later while the "family" was on the move from Bethel to Ephrath. Rachel died after giving birth to Benjamin.

Joseph's family surely was a curious and confusing group—and gives new meaning to the term *extended family!* Joseph probably knew that his father had preferred Rachel to his other wife Leah. He likewise must have guessed that he and his brother Benjamin were his father's favorites—a fact that would have only intensified when Rachel died. This was a family steeped in rivalry—first between the wives, and then between the children.

Undoubtedly, Joseph was also aware of God's promise to his father that from him would arise a great nation: "I will surely make you prosper and will make your descendants like the sand of the sea, which cannot be counted" (Genesis 32:12). This must have been an exciting thought to Joseph, especially as he thought what that prophecy might mean for him someday.

JOSEPH'S TRIP TO EGYPT

There were several reasons why Joseph's brothers had a natural dislike for him. First, the text says that his father liked him best "because he had been born to him in his old age" (Genesis 37:3). As an evidence of his great love, Jacob gave Joseph a richly ornamented robe. "When his brothers saw their father loved him more than any of them, they hated [Joseph] and could not speak a kind word to him" (verse 4). Certainly his brothers were aware of the contest that existed between Leah and Rachel and their handmaidens. Even without the gift of the robe to Joseph, animosity likely was present toward him.

Second, even though his brothers didn't go out of their way to speak to Joseph, Joseph didn't lose opportunities to talk with them, especially to tell them about, his dreams wherein he usually ended up in positions or situations superior to theirs. And "they hated him all the more" (verse 8). In spite of their hatred, Joseph continued to tell them about other similar dreams. He also told his father about his dreams and even Jacob was somewhat incredulous about them.

The record notes that when Joseph was seventeen, he was tending the flocks with his brothers. Not pleased with their behavior, he brought a bad report about them to his father. Some might say this made him a "tattletale." Joseph's actions did not go unnoticed by his brothers.

The older boys apparently felt that some drastic action needed to be taken against Joseph. Little brother was becoming a real pain in the ankle. They decided rather than kill him to sell him to the Ishmaelites, who, his brothers guessed, would take him to Egypt where he would be sold as a slave. This plan fit their brand of "righteousness." They would tell their father that Joseph was killed by a wild animal and would show their father his bloodied robe to prove it. The plan worked, and the brothers assumed they were forever rid of kid brother Joseph.

PREPARATION IN PRISON

While Joseph's preparation for leadership began long before he got to Egypt, it moved into high gear once he arrived. Even though Joseph was in a new culture and faced with a language he hadn't had much (or perhaps any) experience with, he made the best of the situation. Perhaps he had a sense of adventure as he began his new life.

He was purchased as a slave by one of Pharaoh's officials, a man named Potiphar. Joseph's efforts were both productive and visible to his master: "The Lord was with him . . . and gave him success in everything he did" (Genesis 39:3). Potiphar put Joseph in charge of all that he owned and God blessed Potiphar because of Joseph.

Because he was young and handsome, Joseph was noticed by Potiphar's wife. One day when the two of them were alone, she pleaded with him, "Come to bed with me." Joseph resisted and fled from the room, leaving his cloak behind. Having her invitation spurned, Mrs. Potiphar framed Joseph. Her husband, naturally irate, put him in prison, the prison "where the king's prisoners were confined" (verse 20), otherwise referred to as "the house of the captain of the guard." Once again, God was with Joseph and blessed all of his efforts there. He was eventually put in charge of all the prisoners.

Some time later Joseph was assigned to attend Pharaoh's baker and cupbearer, who had been thrown into prison for offending Pharaoh. While there, they each had dreams they couldn't interpret. Joseph, attributing dream interpretations to God, gave them interpretations which came true. He asked the cupbearer (the baker was hanged) to remember him to Pharaoh so that he could be released from prison—a request that was forgotten, at least for a while.

What triggered the cupbearer's memory was a dream by Pharaoh, which he could remember but which no one could interpret. The cupbearer then remembered Joseph and told Pharaoh about him; thus it was that Pharaoh sent for Joseph. When Joseph had been cleaned up and given new clothes for his meeting, Pharaoh told Joseph the dream—a dream about future abundance for Egypt followed by severe famine.

After Joseph had given God's interpretation, and while he still "had the floor," he immediately launched into a detailed plan as to how the "feast and famine" project could be handled. Pharaoh and his officials were so impressed with Joseph's plan of action that Joseph, now thirty years old, was made the prime minister, second in charge only to Pharaoh (41:46).

During the famine Joseph's brothers came to buy food. In one of Scripture's most moving stories (Genesis 42–50),

Joseph dealt with his brothers, testing their hearts and their motives. Once satisfied that indeed they had changed for the better, he revealed his identity to them in an emotion-charged setting, extending them forgiveness and restoration. He then brought them, their possessions, and their families, along with his aged father Jacob, to Egypt where they lived through and beyond the famine.

LEADERSHIP LESSONS FROM JOSEPH

We can learn many things about leading and following from Joseph. I want to suggest but several.

1. *Joseph was consumed by an enduring vision which he believed was from God.* As a dreamer, he was convinced that God was going to do something great with his life sometime in the future. And he was driven by this sense of expectation, this God-given dream. In Joyce Landorf's fascinating novel *Joseph*, we get a sense of Joseph's awareness of that dream: "Long ago God gave me dreams, plans, all designed by Him. My mother called them high and holy dreams. I do not know when they will come to fulfillment, or how, but I must not betray those dreams."[1] And it was the God of those dreams that Joseph followed.

Like Joseph, leaders tend to be consumed by a dream or vision. Calvin Miller observes that "no great leadership ever exists without the power of vision."[2] But the vision has to be nurtured and cared for. It must be kept alive. It must be recognized for what it is, a vision that may, in His good time, be fulfilled, through our efforts or through those of others. But it is *His* vision.

2. *Joseph made the most of every opportunity.* As a slave, he was positive and did his best for the glory of God. In prison, he did his best for the glory of God. When Pharaoh asked him to interpret the dream, Joseph also took advantage of the opportunity to share his plan for dealing with coming famine. And God blessed those efforts.

Most of us would be tempted to complain about mistreatment by our brothers, slavery, false accusations, imprisonment, and separation from family. I'm sure Joseph must have been disappointed or perhaps disillusioned by his unfair mistreatment at times. But he wasn't consumed by it. He made the most of less than ideal circumstances. *Sometimes the best opportunities for leadership come to us disguised as impossible situations.* Yet with God's help those circumstances can be turned around.

When I was at a summer program at Harvard in the early '80s, a group of colleagues gathered to ask us what it was like to be college presidents. Interestingly, the more we talked the more it became clear to me that many saw the presidency as a role more than as an opportunity for leadership. These presidential aspirants all wanted to be presidents of well-established, well-funded, overenrolled institutions that quite frankly needed only a caretaker, not a leader, as president. I argued that some of the best opportunities for leadership existed at colleges and universities which were less-established, under-funded, and under-enrolled. It is at schools like these where abundant challenges exist to "make the most of opportunities."

3. *Joseph paid attention to matters of the heart and did not neglect doing small things well.* We tend to order the activities of our lives around our perception of the activity's importance, and that usually is determined by who's watching. If we are at important functions or if important people are with us, we tend to be very careful about what we do. We are on our best behavior.

Joseph's spirituality, not other people, determined his behavior. Whether dealing with temptation, working as a slave, or serving others in prison, he did it all for the glory of God. Paul said that is a good practice for all of us: "So whether you eat or drink or whatever you do, do it all for the glory of God" (1 Corinthians 10:31). Inasmuch as Joseph did not adjust his behavior to satisfy a human audience, whether constituents or donors or some other influential group, all of his moments became noticeable moments or at least worthy of notice.

We tend sometimes to not pay attention to small things, whether money or behavior. Interestingly, Jesus taught with regard to money that faithfulness in small things translates, at least in God's eyes, as faithfulness in large matters (Luke 16:10-12). And our faithfulness in most, if not all, of life is largely determined by the condition of our hearts.

4. *Joseph did well in his task as prime minister.* Earlier we discussed Joseph's vision, his willingness to depend on God in all that he did. Just as important, however, is the fact that Joseph achieved the purposes which brought him to office in the first place. He managed well the seven years of plenty and the seven years of famine. Too often in leadership books, the emphasis on how to lead tends to overshadow the importance of needing to complete the actual leadership task. While the means to the end are important, we still have to pay attention to the ends.

One of the reasons many leaders resist quantification of any leadership goal or assignment is that quantification allows for measurement or assessment. And measurement permits accountability. And whether they admit it or not, many leaders do not want accountability, for accountability provides the potential for failure. And leaders dislike failure. Many boards, unfortunately, sometimes accept a pleasing personality in lieu of acceptable performance of the leadership task. This is not a call for leaders who have an unpleasant personality. It is a call to say that effective leaders must have more than just a pleasing personality or nice credentials; they have to effect movement toward achievement of the organization's purpose.

5. *Joseph patiently followed God's time clock for his life.* One never senses in Joseph's story that somehow he thought God's clock was slow. Indeed, one has the pervasive feeling that God's plan was right on schedule, even though Joseph could not see what God was doing. How different is this story from that of Joseph's great grandfather Abraham, who sensed a need to help God speed things up and so had a child by Sarah's handmaiden Hagar.

Landorf notes what might have been Joseph's reaction to God's timing in his life:

> It was all a part of His time of seasoning for me. I took my apprenticeship in living when I was thrown into that dungeon. The first day of the iron chains, and in the darkness of that place, I asked myself, "Has this happened to me *without* God's knowledge or consent?" And . . . my heart resounded with, "No! *He* knows and consented." So, I reasoned, He must have a plan! But at that time I never had a dream, a sign; nor did I have any solid proof that He was

working . . . only a quiet confidence that He *was!* . . . It pleased God to make me a slave, a prisoner, and an interpreter, for in His time He brought me to Pharaoh.[3]

I know of few leaders who have not been frustrated with God's sense of timing in their leadership task or in their personal lives. "Where is God now?" we ask. One of the things that God continues to teach me about His sense of timing is to make me ask myself the question, "What else is there in this that He wants me to learn?" Patience with God's timing is one of the really tough responsibilities of leadership. And once again, it requires me to be a follower, to stay in touch with His leading. I need to continue to remind myself of verses like Habakkuk 2:3 (TLB): "But these things I plan won't happen right away. Slowly, steadily, surely, the time approaches when the vision will be fulfilled. If it seems slow, do not despair, for these things will surely come to pass. Just be patient! They will not be overdue a single day!"

6. *Joseph was willing to forgive those who did him wrong.* Never in the text do we read that once Joseph was placed in a position of leadership he went back and got even against all those who had wronged him, whether Egyptians or members of his own family. While he did put his brothers through a series of wrenching tests in order to know their hearts, once they had passed the tests he extended forgiveness and reconciliation. Indeed, he gave them not only the food they requested of him, but went far beyond, moving them all to Egypt to survive the famine.

Joseph's example of forgiveness is a necessary one for all leaders to model. In answering affirmatively his inquiry, "Can a leader survive a visible mistake?" Calvin Miller says:

A leader must seek as gold . . . a spirit of forgiveness toward followers who, from time to time, will sin. When Jesus said, "In everything, do to others what you would have them do to you" (Matthew 7:12), He was not merely stating a nice principle of life. He was stating a key truth that applies to every arena of leadership. A follower you treat with charity is far more prone to forgive you when you are caught in a storm of contempt.[4]

And so it must be when we deal with the leader and forgiveness.

7. *Joseph saw the hand of God in his circumstances; he saw the big picture, from God's perspective.* This quality is essential for Christian leaders. Joseph was involved in more than merely playing the number-two political role in Egypt. He was doing more than simply helping people survive a difficult famine. He was doing more than merely extending forgiveness to his brothers. Rather, it appears that he was aware of how God was using him to achieve *His* larger purpose.

For example, what was really behind Joseph's severe tests of his brothers? Why was it important for him to know their hearts? Why did he give Benjamin more than the others? Again, Landorf suggests one plausible reason. Joseph was concerned that "unless his brothers had changed, the death of his father would mean a bitter family dispute over their inheritance, and the family of Israel would not emerge as a great nation but as a pitifully shattered remnant of a family."[5]

Joseph himself seemed to have been aware of his role in the preservation of human life. After he had shown himself to his brothers, he told them not to be angry for what they had done to him, for God all along was working out His higher purpose: "It was to save lives that God sent me ahead of you. . . . So then, it was not you who sent me here, but God" (Genesis 45:5, 8). After Jacob died, and Joseph's brothers became afraid that Joseph would now take his revenge against them, Joseph once again displayed his awareness of this higher purpose: "You intended to harm me, but God intended it for good to accomplish what is now being done, the saving of many lives" (50:20).

Joseph was willing to be a follower before he experienced leadership. He was willing to be led by the Heavenly Father through places and in paths he himself certainly wouldn't have chosen. Joseph was prepared to lead because he was also prepared to follow. And he was aware of God's greater purpose in his life: "God has sent this Hebrew into the land of Egypt to keep you and your families alive so that one day we shall survive as the children of Israel and be a great nation of people."[6]

SIMILARITIES BETWEEN JOSEPH AND DANIEL

Whereas the Scripture provides us with a rich history of Joseph's family background, we are told precious little about Daniel. Nonetheless, we can see some clear and common parallels in their lives.

For example, both Joseph and Daniel came from well-to-do families, and if not well-to-do, certainly above average. This afforded certain privileges and opportunities that otherwise would not have been available to them. Second, both were probably in their teens when they were separated from their families and carried off to a foreign country and a culture different from their own. Third, it would appear that both were very able and intelligent young men. Joseph moved quickly through the ranks to leadership, whether in Potiphar's house, the king's prison, or Pharaoh's court. Daniel, along with his friends—Shadrach, Meshach, and Abednego—were at the top of their class in the "University of Babylon." Scripture notes that they were "in every matter of wisdom and understanding . . . ten times better than all the magicians . . . in the whole kingdom" (Daniel 1:20). There are additional parallels.

Both had a God-given ability to interpret dreams. And this ability led almost immediately to a high position in secular government, in Egypt and Babylon respectively. Each was given at a relatively young age major leadership responsibilities for hundreds of thousands of people.

Interestingly, when Joseph served in Egypt, God had a servant of His choosing in a position to help preserve the fledgling family of Israel from being destroyed by a famine. Hundreds of years later, during the Jewish exile, God had Daniel in a similar key position of influence in the Babylonian government. As one commentator has observed: "Right at the beginning of Israel's history God had His man—Joseph—at the Egyptian court. Now again, at this crisis-point, God placed Daniel in a position of influence at the political center of the Babylonian Empire, for the whole period of the exile."[7]

The only other parallel I will note here is that both Joseph and Daniel appear to have persevered in their faithfulness to God to the end of their lifetimes. Often initial spiritual brilliance is marred by a defection from the faith in later years. The example of Solomon is but one that comes to mind. Alert and vibrant faith in God over a lifetime of service ought to be a goal for all Christian leaders.

DANIEL AND LEADERSHIP

We could draw numerous observations about leadership from Daniel's long period of success in the political world. We have time only to address several.

1. *Daniel had a consistent walk with God.* He was a faithful follower of the Lord and this faith anchored his leadership. At every available opportunity Daniel gave credit to God for all He had done for him. As a young man we see Daniel standing before powerful King Nebuchadnezzar stating that it is God in heaven who reveals mysteries (Daniel 2:28). In his old age we see Daniel as a man of prayer despite government policy (6:10), testifying to God's faithfulness before King Darius (verses 21-22). That God saw Daniel as a righteous man is seen in Ezekiel 14:14, a verse we previously noted.

2. *Daniel was a quick learner.* That is, he was "quick to understand" (Daniel 1:4). We see this in his formal education; in his speech reflecting "wisdom and tact" to Arioch; in his responses to kings; and in his management success. Daniel was a quick study. The text notes, for example, that Daniel had duly impressed King Darius: "Now Daniel so distinguished himself among the administrators ... by his exceptional qualities that the king planned to set him over the whole kingdom" (6:3).

Effective leaders have the capacity to digest large amounts of information, both of a cognitive and of an intuitive nature, in a short period of time. When a new leader arrives, unless the "organizational ship is rapidly sinking," which usually means quick action needs to be taken, it is imperative to learn much before premature action is taken. While it is important that facts be mastered, it is equally important that the organizational culture be understood and assimilated and that significant organizational values be internalized.

3. *Daniel was loyal to his king* (even though he seldom reported to godly ones). Nebuchadnezzar, Belshazzar,

and Darius each considered Daniel an important member of the leadership team and rewarded him with prestige accordingly. Each king also recognized and appreciated Daniel's faithfulness to his God. Nebuchadnezzar's testimony may be directly attributable to Daniel: "Now I, Nebuchadnezzar, praise and exalt and glorify the King of heaven, because everything He does is right and all His ways are just. And those who walk in pride He is able to humble" (4:37). But one seldom gets the sense that Daniel was only a "yes" man before his kings, maintaining before Darius, for example, "Nor have I ever done any wrong before you, O king" (6:22).

Loyal and faithful service to one's employer is seldom discussed in leadership books but I believe it is wrongly neglected. Whether a chief executive officer hired by a board, whether a pastor called by the people, whether a line administrator reporting to another, leaders owe loyalty where it is due. As Daniel and Joseph both illustrate, working in secular employment provides no excuse to be disloyal. Leaders at every level need to be able to say, as did Daniel, to those to whom they are accountable, "I have never done any wrong before you." If I believe I can't be loyal to my employer, then I have the responsibility to seek employment elsewhere. (For more on this matter, refer to chapter 5 of my book *The Other Side of Leadership*.)

4. *Daniel was willing to pay the price to be godly.* The best example of this is Daniel's unwillingness to give up his prayer life in order to obey the laws of the Medes and Persians. As you may recall, Daniel's colleagues were so jealous of his success that they conspired to have the king create a law that prohibited prayer to anyone but the king. Interestingly, Daniel's political enemies were so impressed with the consistency in his prayer life that they knew such a law would surely lead to Daniel's downfall. They knew that they would "never find any basis for charges against this man Daniel unless it has something to do with the law of his God" (6:5).

They were right. The law was passed. Daniel, surely by now a senior statesman, predictably didn't obey it and as a result he was thrown into a den of lions. But God sent an angel to protect Daniel, and as a result, "when Daniel was lifted from the den, no wound was found on him, because he had trusted in his God" (verse 23). Many a leader knows what it is like to be "thrown to lions." Rarely has it been for an act of obedience to the Heavenly King.

Often when we are called to take a stand for godliness, we have no idea what the outcome will be. While Daniel undoubtedly hoped God would protect him in the lions' den, he had no advance assurance that God would do so. When Daniel's three friends were thrown into the fiery furnace, they willingly went, not knowing in advance that God would protect them. As Hebrews 11 makes clear, sometimes protection is granted; at other times it is not. No matter. What is important is that the price for godliness in leadership is always worth paying.

Maintaining a walk by faith may always be costly. And our Christian brothers and sisters in Third World countries know the reality of this truth better than do those of us in North America. So, if in our places of employment and in our positions of leadership we are asked to choose between God or Caesar, my hope is that we would have the courage to pay whatever price necessary and choose to be godly. That's always the choice that pays the best eternal dividends.

QUESTIONS FOR FURTHER THOUGHT AND DISCUSSION

1. These are but two of many biblical characters who held key positions of leadership in a secular government. What others come to mind? How were their roles similar or dissimilar to those of Joseph and Daniel? Esther and Nehemiah are but two suggestions to get you started.
2. Some have suggested that Daniel and his friends made their "we can go no further than this" stand over diet and drink (Daniel 1:8-16). Why do you think they drew the line at this point rather than at having to learn the less-than-God-honoring pagan literature? Is not what goes into the mind just as important as what goes into the stomach?
3. As we have seen, both Joseph and Daniel were taken from their families during their youth. In their new countries, they

received little or no support for their Jewish faith. How did they survive? What role might their parents have played? Would your teenagers in an equivalent situation fare just as well as these?

4. It appears that Joseph (see Genesis 41:45) was given an Egyptian wife. Was she a believer? Did he make a wise choice in agreeing to this marriage? Did he have a choice? What would you have recommended that he do?

5. Joseph's testing of his brothers was quite strenuous. He didn't hesitate to put them in jail when it served his purpose. Initially, he jailed them all for three days. Simeon was put in jail for a longer period until they returned the second time to buy grain. Joseph kept tricking them by giving them back their money and by planting his other personal items in their grain sacks. If you had experienced what Joseph had experienced at the hand of his brothers, how would you have responded to them? What would you have done differently, if anything?

6. Clearly both Daniel and Joseph were gifted administrators and executives. Where did they learn leadership? If you were to develop a leadership training program and could base it only on what we know of the lives of Joseph and Daniel, what key elements would you include? Which would you omit?

7. Both Daniel and Joseph were given a variety of what we might call "leadership" tests, tests concerning such things as sexual purity, faithfulness in small things, the willingness to forgive, and dealing with adverse circumstances. If you were to create a series of tests potential contemporary leaders should face, what would they be and why?

8. As you look at the way Joseph carried out his responsibilities for Pharaoh, would you say he acted with justice? See, for example, Genesis 47:21: "And Joseph reduced the people to servitude, from one end of Egypt to the other."

CHAPTER
TWELVE

PETER AND PAUL

Thus far in our study of biblical leaders, we have looked at the Old Testament. There is a good reason for this. In many cases, the Old Testament provides more complete background information on its "actors" than does the New Testament. In the New Testament, aside from what we learn from the Gospels and from the Book of Acts, the other primary source of information comes from what the actors themselves tell us.

We could start with any of the twelve Apostles, for example. As a young man, I was particularly interested in Timothy and the instruction he was given by Paul. And then there is Barnabas, that early leader of the church. Priscilla and Aquila played key roles in Paul's ministry. There are others.

I have settled on just two: Peter and Paul. First, Peter and Paul greatly influenced the early church, perhaps more so than any others. Peter played a significant role in the Jerusalem church and in his missionary journeys. Paul, through his varied missionary journeys, was instrumental in seeing Christianity spread around the then known world.

My approach will be first to provide some background on each. I will then follow up by showing some of the similarities and differences in their lives and ministries, identifying several key points which I believe are relevant for our study in leadership. For helpful background on Peter and Paul I have read a number of handbooks and encyclopedias. I have found John Pollock's book, *The Apostle*,[1] to be particularly useful. Both Peter and Paul provide limited background about themselves in their writings.

THE LIFE OF PAUL

Born around the time of Christ, Paul claimed to be "a Jew of Tarsus, a citizen of no mean city, of the people of Israel, of the tribe of Benjamin, a Hebrew born of Hebrews."[2] His given name was Saul. His family was probably quite wealthy. His father was "most likely . . . a master tentmaker."[3] The argument for wealth is based on the fact that Paul's family were citizens of Rome, something that was possible at that time only for a large sum of money or in recognition of rendering significant services to Rome.[4] "Roman citizenship conferred local distinction and hereditary privileges which each member could claim wherever he traveled throughout the empire."[5]

The city of Paul's childhood was a kind of melting pot, a "fusion of civilizations at peace under the rule of Rome."[6] As good Pharisees, however, his parents took great care to ensure that the family was not contaminated by friendships with Gentile children. Even though Paul "could speak Greek . . . and had a working knowledge of Latin, his family at home spoke Aramaic, the language of Judea, a derivative of Hebrew."[7] It was a nationalistic family, one that valued "the high honor of being Israelites" over being "freemen of Tarsus and Roman citizens."[8]

"By his thirteenth birthday, Paul had mastered Jewish history, the poetry of the psalms, and the majestic literature of the prophets."[9] Wanting the best for his family, Paul was sent by his parents to Jerusalem, where, "during the next five or six years, he sat at the feet of Gamaliel, grandson of Hillel, the supreme teacher."[10] There he "learned to debate in the question-and-answer style known . . . as the 'diatribe,' and to expound, for a rabbi was not only part preacher but part lawyer, who prosecuted or defended those who broke the sacred law."[11] Paul's performance as a student would ultimately land him a seat in the Sanhedrin. Given the fact that Israel was a theocracy, the members of the Sanhedrin were "equally judges, senators, and spiritual masters."[12]

What probably led Paul back home from Jerusalem was his need to master a trade, "for every Jew was bred to a trade and in theory no rabbi took fees but rather supported himself."[13] And while Paul was now steeped in learning, he had not yet mastered any trade. The family business, tentmaking, was Paul's logical choice of trade. While learning it, Paul was most likely active in the synagogue. Undoubtedly, his parents were proud of Paul and of his accomplishments. "Paul's father could take full and justified delight in this son who had followed in his steps as a Pharisee and had the intellectual force to reach the highest office in Israel."[14] Shortly after "his thirtieth birthday, Paul returned to Jerusalem . . . (where) his days were consumed by his legal career and grooming himself for heaven."[15] Paul probably thought that one of his new tasks in Jerusalem might involve refuting the claims of the new Jesus sect he had undoubtedly heard about.

The first time we see Paul in Acts he is involved with the stoning of Stephen. People not only laid their clothes at his feet, the text says, "Saul was there, giving approval to his [Stephen's] death" (Acts 8:1). Having done this, "Saul began to destroy the church. Going from house to house, he dragged off men and women and put them in prison" (verse 3). Paul "charged like an animal tearing its prey. This was not the sad efficiency of an officer obeying distasteful orders; the heart was engaged; and the mind too, with the thoroughness of an inquisitor unmasking treason, until Paul's operations had reduced a vigorous citywide community to apparent impotence, its leaders fled or in hiding."[16] Apparently not content with harming the "Way" only in Jerusalem, Paul diligently pursued persecution of Christ's followers in Damascus. And it was on the way to Damascus that Jesus confronted Saul the persecutor and transformed him into Paul the apostle.

His encounter on the road to Damascus is recorded in Acts 9. When a voice from heaven demanded of Paul, "Why do you persecute Me?" Paul wanted to know who was speaking to him. The voice replied, "I am Jesus, whom you are persecuting." I like Pollock's version of what Paul must have felt about this supernatural confrontation: "Then Paul knew. In a second that seemed an eternity he saw the wounds in Jesus' hands and feet, saw the face and knew that he had seen the Lord, that He was alive, as Stephen and the others had said, and that He loved not only those whom Paul persecuted but Paul. . . . Not one word of reproach. . . . Instantaneously, he was shatteringly aware that he had been fighting Jesus."[17]

Later, while awaiting a visit from Ananias, Paul had time to reflect on how he had persecuted Jesus: "Nor was it only murder and cruelty. He had blasphemed and insulted and persecuted the Lord, whose response had been to seek him out and show him a love which surpassed anything he had known. The more he bathed himself in this love . . . the more he was broken down by the enormity of what he had done."[18] Paul immediately began to experience the forgiveness that has characterized new creatures in Christ down through the ages, something Paul would later write about in 1 Corinthians.

Following his conversion it appears that Paul went into Arabia, where for a period of time he was taught directly by the Lord. It wasn't until three years had passed that Paul finally presented himself in Jerusalem, to Peter. Pollock analogizes Paul's desert experience to that of Moses and of Jesus Himself.[19] Following his return from the desert, Paul over the next twenty to thirty years became a world traveler, clear in his focus to share the good news to both Jews and Gentiles, and to establish churches. Even though he was not then aware of his role in shaping the future history of the world, or of his impact on the church, this man endured countless persecutions for the sake of spreading the Gospel.

In his second letter to the Corinthians, for example, Paul recounts some of his sufferings for the name of Jesus:

I have worked much harder, been in prison more frequently, been flogged more severely, and been exposed to death again and again. Five times I received from the Jews the forty lashes minus one. Three times I was beaten with rods, once I was stoned, three times I was shipwrecked, I spent a night and a day in the open sea, I have been constantly on the move. I have been in danger from rivers, in danger from bandits, in danger from my own countrymen, in danger from Gentiles; in danger in the city, in danger in the country, in danger at sea; and in danger from false brothers. I have labored and toiled and have often gone without sleep; I have known hunger and thirst and have often gone without food; I have been cold and naked (2 Corinthians 11:23-27).

He told these same readers, "We are hard pressed on every side, but not crushed; perplexed, but not in despair; persecuted, but not abandoned; struck down, but not destroyed" (4:8).

Yet he was able to say, as he approached his last years, that "I have fought the good fight, I have finished the race, I have kept the faith" (2 Timothy 4:7).

PETER

We learn much about Peter from the Gospels. Mark notes that after John the Baptist was put in prison, Jesus was walking beside the Sea of Galilee, and saw Simon and his brother Andrew fishing, "for they were fishermen" (Mark 1:16). Jesus told them, "Follow Me," and He would make them fishers of men—and they at once left to follow Jesus. (A similar story is told by Matthew and Luke.) As a fisherman, Peter would not have been known for his education or his social graces. When Jesus said, "Follow," Peter followed.

While Mark, Luke, and Matthew note the time when Peter followed Jesus, John recounts (chapter 1) perhaps the time when Peter first met Jesus. Apparently Peter's brother Andrew (and others) were impressed with the preaching of John the Baptist. Yet when John identified Jesus as the Lamb of God, Andrew followed Jesus instead. After meeting Jesus, the first thing Andrew did was to find his brother Simon and bring him to Jesus. Jesus immediately added to his name, calling him Cephas or Peter.

As we follow Peter through the Gospels, we see him as rather outspoken and in the limelight. For example, Peter was the one who wanted to walk on the water (Matthew 14:28). It was Peter who boldly confessed Jesus as the Christ and on whom Christ said He would build His church (16:16-18). It was Peter who insisted Jesus didn't know what He was talking about when Jesus announced His upcoming death (16:22). Jesus had to rebuke him. It was

Peter who wanted to build shelters in honor of what he had seen at the Transfiguration (17:4). It was Peter who wanted clarification on how much he was supposed to forgive (18:21). It was Peter, perhaps because he was seen as an important disciple, who was approached regarding payment of the temple tax (17:24). It was Peter who had the sword and who cut off the ear of the high priest's servant (John 18:10). And it was Peter who, with James and John, appeared to be part of Jesus' "inner circle." For example, it was these three disciples who went with Jesus to the Mount of Transfiguration; who were with Him when He healed Jairus' daughter; and when He prayed on Gethsemane.

Peter was also that disciple who Jesus identified as the one who would verbally deny Him three times. Jesus told Peter, "Satan has asked to sift you as wheat. But I have prayed for you, Simon, that your faith may not fail. And when you have turned back, strengthen your brothers" (Luke 22:31-32). Peter did indeed deny Jesus three times just as the Lord predicted, and afterward he wept bitterly. Jesus gently restored Peter in His marvelous encounter with him recorded in John 21.

The Peter we see in the Book of Acts appears to be a different kind of person than the one we see in the Gospels. Once he was a hot-air, want-to-be-in-the-middle-of-things, take-charge type of person. No longer. No more, "Lord, I'll never desert You" statements. No more "You'll not wash my feet" rebukes. Peter has been broken, and the Peter we see in Acts has a renewed heart, one that has been forgiven by the Saviour.

Peter, however, continued to play a key role after the ascension of Christ. In Acts 1 we see him offering advice for choosing a replacement for Judas. In Acts 2 we see him, newly empowered by the Holy Spirit, preaching a sermon at which about 3,000 responded. In Acts 3 he heals a cripple. As a result, he is confronted by an angry Sanhedrin. He reminds them that he has a higher obligation to obey God than to obey them. Even those who witnessed Peter's powerful defense were impressed: "When they saw the courage of Peter and John and realized that they were unschooled, ordinary men, they were astonished and *they took note that these men had been with Jesus*" (Acts 4:13, emphasis mine).

There was one more event of significance that dramatically shaped Peter, and that was the vision he experienced in Caesarea (Acts 10). In that vision God made it clear that the Gospel message was no longer limited only to the Jews. And so it was with great joy that Peter shared the good news about Jesus with the Gentile Cornelius. Criticized for this action, he later made a powerful defense of his actions in Jerusalem. At the still later Council of Jerusalem, he again made a key speech which helped lead to a lessening of the requirements of the Jewish Law for Gentile Christians. Nevertheless, Peter saw his primary mission to be that of preaching to the Jews (Galatians 2:7).

Paul and Peter apparently crossed paths early in Paul's Christian walk. Paul notes that on one of his first visits to Jerusalem as a Christian, he spent fifteen days with Peter, no doubt as a "spiritual student." Even though at times they disagreed (Acts 2:11-14), over the years the two developed a mutually encouraging friendship. Peter calls him "our dear brother Paul" in his second letter (2 Peter 3:15), even though in that same passage he also acknowledged that some of Paul's letters contain some things that are hard to understand. At the end of their lives, Pollock notes that they may have been in prison together for some time, "possibly as much as nine months."[20] Tradition has it that they both were executed on the same day, Peter, "nailed to a cross as a public spectacle at Nero's Circus on the Vatican, head downward at his own request, and Paul, as a Roman citizen, beheaded in a less public place."[21]

COMMON BACKGROUND ELEMENTS: PETER AND PAUL

We often tend to isolate the events and people of the early church from the events and people of the Gospels. We sometimes forget, for example, that Peter and Paul were contemporaries of Jesus, even though Peter didn't meet Jesus until probably his late twenties. While Paul undoubtedly had heard of Jesus, he had never met Him until their encounter on the Damascus road. Paul and Peter shared several common experiences.

First, they appeared at about the same time in history and for about the same number of years. *Second*, while they came from dissimilar backgrounds, each spent a significant amount of time with Jesus, Peter as a disciple and Paul taught by Jesus in Arabia. Each had a clear vision of the Saviour. *Third,* each had significant confrontations with the Lord that led to brokenness and further usefulness for Him. Paul's confrontation came on the road to Damascus; for Peter it was after he had denied Christ three times. As each reflected on the magnitude of his sin (for Paul, murder and blasphemy and for Peter, flat-out denial of the Lord), they were made ready for God's future use. When Paul was introduced to Ananias, he was no longer the hotshot lawyer who thought only about himself, his righteous efforts, and about how lucky God was to have him on His team. Peter was no longer the braggadocian fisherman. *Fourth,* each experienced hardship, persecution, and suffering for the sake of the Gospel. *Fifth,* each was willing to make major changes in his belief system, as both became open to the Gentiles receiving the Gospel.

LEADERSHIP THEMES: PETER AND PAUL

It is extremely difficult to limit observations about leadership in the lives of Peter and Paul. Their letters teach us volumes about the attitude of the heart, the role of service, and the power of Christ in us as leaders both to will and to do His good pleasure. Paul repeatedly emphasized that it was "not I but Christ" who was at work in him and obviously the one who needs to be at work in us. Regardless of the difficulty of the task in identifying only a few observations, let's begin. These are not intended to be inclusive and are not listed in any order of priority.

First, it is imperative in leadership that we *experience brokenness in our lives, and then live afterward as people who have been overcome and overwhelmed by the Saviour's love.* As we have noted, both Peter and Paul came to a point in their lives where Jesus broke their "me-ness" and transformed them into persons consumed by the Saviour's love. Peter had lived with the Saviour for three years, and I'm sure had been used of Him. Nevertheless, he had apparently never been broken for the Saviour. Paul was consumed by his quest for righteousness and his love for God. But somehow he had missed being transformed by the Saviour.

181

When we live as broken people, we will have experienced and will continue to experience several things. For example, as broken people, *we will recognize the ugliness of sin of any kind* and *recognize how it keeps us away from fellowship with Jesus.* Too often, we live under the false assumption that we are basically righteous people. We tell ourselves that we sin, but only "once in a while," and usually then the "sin" is something "minor." We fail to understand that with Jesus, there are no "minor" sins, only sin.

For example, He groups together sexual immorality with greed, murder with envy, and theft with arrogance (Mark 7:20-23). Only as we see ourselves as people who have never merited the grace and love of God, as people who daily need to experience His forgiveness, only then will we see ourselves as Jesus sees us—people continually forgiven by Him and continually clothed with His righteousness, not our own.

As my wife Marylou and I have personally wrestled with this issue of brokenness in our own lives, we have observed that too often, in the church and in other Christian organizations, we live under the myth of organizational perfectionism rather than under the reality of forgiveness. We want to see employees in the organization as perfect people, rather than as imperfect people in constant need of His forgiveness. We want to see ourselves as having no problems or questions but all of the answers.

Rebecca Pippert reflects on this concern, noting that before her conversion, it was "pious behavior that made me want to run for the hills. In fact, when I came close to the faith, I wavered before making a commitment because I was afraid such 'holy' behavior would be required of me. If this were the case, I knew I was in big trouble because no matter how devout I'd become there was no way I could pull it off."[22] Pippert recalls the answer of G.K. Chesterton to the question, "'What is the Problem in the Universe?': 'I am.' Sincerely, G.K. Chesterton."[23] She further notes her conversations with a recovering alcoholic about why he seldom went to church during his alcoholic days: "Let me tell you about the times I went to church during my drinking days. The message was always very polite but firm:

come back when you have your act together." Pippert then asked him why the church isn't like an AA (Alcoholics Anonymous) meeting: "Because we [the church] don't really believe that the problem rests in us. We think the problem is 'out there'; we are good and respectable in here [the church]. We do not admit that the rot is in us too."[24]

Why is it that throughout the Scriptures, Jesus targeted His most severe condemnations to the religious community? While He told the woman caught in the act of adultery to "go and sin no more," it was also in essence the same message He extended to Paul and to Peter at their moments of failure. Why is it Jesus constantly told the people He ministered to that their sins were forgiven? Perhaps it is because the theme of the cross, of the empty tomb, of the Gospel is precisely that—the powerful message of forgiveness. And brokenness requires being forgiven.

The reality of leadership is that both leaders and followers are all forgiven people. And the reality of being forgiven by the Saviour for sin, whether "big or small," is simply overwhelming. Perhaps brokenness reflects the recognition not only of the price paid by the Saviour for sin, but also of His incredible love for us that took Him to the cross.

Living as broken leaders also means that we will not only be continually consumed by the recognition of the Saviour's love for us but we will also respond gratefully to the Saviour's desire that we be *consumed with our love for Him*. While we sometimes get mixed up in our "doing" priorities for Jesus, He makes it perfectly clear what our most important priorities should be: "Love the Lord your God with all your heart and with all your soul and with all your mind. This is the first and greatest commandment" (Matthew 22:37-38). He told His disciples to "seek first His kingdom and His righteousness" (6:33). It's not that we are not to pursue doing justice or other good things. It's just that what we do must first flow out of our love for the Saviour. As John expressed it, "We love Him because He first loved us" (1 John 4:19). Henri Nouwen refers to this as understanding His "first love."[25] This must be at the center of the heart of every leader. This impacts our perspective and vision. It affects how we share. And it certainly gives direction to how we lead and follow.

Our brokenness and forgiveness compels us to extend forgiveness to others within the church or within the organizations we lead. Frankly, we cop out on this one with our expressions of righteous indignation at human failure, knowing full well our own failures. Does this mean we ignore sin? No, I'm not saying that. What it means is that we perhaps have to make far greater efforts at seeking reconciliation, restoration, and rehabilitation when people in our communities sin. Rather than washing our hands of the matter and "removing these sinners from our midst," we must make more diligent attempts to handle these matters biblically, particularly so where brokenness and repentance are evident.

Many have ignored reading Gordon MacDonald's book *Rebuilding Your Broken World*[26] because we self-righteously conclude that since we haven't committed the sin of sexual immorality, his book won't speak to us. I had that same attitude. Having later read his book, I now think it has relevance for dealing with sin of *any* kind. Doesn't sin of any kind need to be rehabilitated? I fail to see the emphasis of Scripture supporting our practical distinctions that only "serious forgiven sin" merits efforts to rehabilitate and restore. If all sin has consequences, those consequences need to be dealt with. Perhaps the reason we make distinctions and have rehabilitation programs only for serious sin is that such a myth permits us to indulge in the continued belief of our own righteousness. Yet whatever righteousness we think we might have within the organization is never our own righteousness but His.

I have enough contact with the secular world to know that one of the reasons many people reject Christ is because the model they see in the church is that only perfect, unbroken people need apply. That is, the world sees how we deal with those of our community who sin. They see our lack of unity and love for one another. They see how we "remove sinners" in order to keep ourselves and our organizations clean and unblemished.

Again, I'm convinced that this kind of corporate self-righteousness is sin itself because it misconstrues not only the message of the "good news" but runs counter to the life, practice, and message of the Saviour: "It is not the healthy who need a doctor, but the sick. I have not come to call the righteous, but sinners to repentance" (Luke 5:32). Again, the way Jesus responded to Peter's sin is powerfully instructive on this point. He was not removed from the "organization" for his sin, something that undoubtedly would have occurred in the contemporary evangelical organization. Rather, Peter was restored quickly and promptly without one word of recorded condemnation from Jesus. That's a pretty incredible and powerful example.

If our need for brokenness is important in leadership, there are indeed other observations about leadership that we learn from Peter and Paul. And this leads to a *second* observation: *Leaders must understand the incredible power of Christian love.* Probably no greater illustration of this love outside of the Gospels exists than Paul's observations on the subject in 1 Corinthians 13:

> *If* I speak in the tongues of men and of angels, but have not love, I am only a resounding gong or a clanging cymbal. *If* I have the gift of prophecy and can fathom all mysteries and all knowledge, and *if* I have a faith that can move mountains, but have not love, I am nothing. *If* I give all I possess to the poor and surrender my body to the flames, but have not love, I gain nothing. Love is patient, love is kind. It does not envy, it does not boast, it is not proud. It is not rude, it is not self-seeking, it is not easily angered, it keeps *no* record of wrongs. Love does not delight in evil but rejoices with truth. It *always* protects, *always* trusts, *always* hopes, *always* perseveres. Love *never* fails. . . . And now these three remain: faith, hope, and love. But the greatest of these is love (verses 1-8, 13, emphasis mine).

Leaders ought to work at and model this kind of love. We must strive to see it practiced in community. Enough said.

Third, leaders need to *understand the incredible power of God, available to us, in and through Christ.* Paul makes incredible efforts to explain Christ's power, particularly in Ephesians and Colossians:

I pray also that the eyes of your heart may be enlightened in order that you may know ... His incomparably great power for us who believe. That power is like the working of His mighty strength, which He exerted in Christ when He raised Him from the dead and seated Him at His right hand in the heavenly realms, far above all rule and authority, power and dominion, and every title that can be given (Ephesians 1:18-21).

For by Him all things were created: things in heaven and on earth, visible and invisible, whether thrones or powers or rulers or authorities; all things were created by Him and for Him. He is before all things, and in Him all things hold together (Colossians 1:16-17).

When leadership models vision and action that reflect an understanding of the incredible power of Christ, when God's power is plainly visible through the lives of people associated with an organization, problems become mere opportunities for God to work. People begin to understand anew His ability to make crooked ways straight. We learn anew what it means to "trust and obey." I don't mean for a moment to suggest that we get everything solved the way we want it. Rather, it means we see the problem through the eyes of the Saviour, and in so doing, give Him the opportunity to intervene on our behalf, however He may choose to do that.

There is a *fourth* observation: Leaders need to *see the empowerment that comes from friendship*. Paul's letters in particular overflow with evidence of his friendships with others. It is not unusual to find him closing a letter with a long listing of greetings to or from his friends. Words like *dear brother* and *dear friend* flow from his pen. The letter to the Colossians is but one example.

In his discussion on Paul's involvement with prayer and friendship, Houston makes the following helpful observations.

Friendship has never been a central theme of Western Christianity. In contrast, the ancient Greeks and Romans made friendship central to their society.... [In the] ... modern world ... friendships are no longer the noblest things in the world. Instead, our careers are the integrating bond of our society. . . . Put . . . bluntly, the pursuit of money and power underlies a great deal of what goes on in the modern world. . . . The disintegration of friendship is a very serious challenge for the credibility of the Christian faith. That is why we should insist that friendship and prayer together reflect the character of God as Father, Son and Holy Spirit. . . . For the rest of Paul's life, his work and his friendships were shot through with prayer. . . . In his own life, prayer and teaching were integrated. . . . The key feature of Paul's prayer life is that it dominates all his relationships with other people. . . . Paul made time for the commitment of friendship, even though he might have been weighted down with his ministry. . . . Paul's friendships went hand-in-hand with the spreading of the Christian message.[27]

Perhaps our inability to develop "true friendship" with the living God flows from our inability or unwillingness to develop friends in leadership. How can we claim to celebrate friendship with Jesus if we haven't learned to celebrate friendship with other people? I've talked with enough leaders to know that not many have a really good friend, let alone really good friends. The demands of the job, or so we convince ourselves, don't allow for friendship. I remain convinced that this is one of the areas of my life in which I need to continue to make some significant changes.

What convicts me further at this point is that Jesus wants our friendship and our fellowship. Indeed, He says it this way: "I no longer call you servants. . . . Instead, I have called you friends, for everything that I learned from the Father I have made known to you" (John 15:15). Paul tells us that God has called us "into fellowship with . . . Jesus" (1 Corinthians 1:9). Peter tells us to "have sincere love for your brothers, love one another deeply, from the heart" (1 Peter 1:22). Without friends we have a chance at survival in leadership. With friends, we will have the opportunity to flourish.

Fifth, we learn from Peter and Paul that the Christian leader understands that *the final destination is not retirement to "Easy Street" but an eternal home in heaven.* That's what makes suffering both bearable and worthwhile. That's why denial of one's self, taking up the cross of Christ, and following Jesus is the Christian way. That's why the leader is willing to make the tough choice, the biblical decision, rather than gaining the applause and recognition of the world at the risk of losing his soul (Mark 8:34-38). Peter reminds us that we are to live our lives here as "strangers" (1 Peter 1:17). The writer of Hebrews uses the phrase "aliens and strangers on earth" (Hebrews 11:13). When we know that our final destination is not the "completion of the fund-raising campaign" or the "last building built," we can set our minds on things above and become freed of our own way to follow Christ in His way. In discussing enemies of the Cross, Paul reminds the Philippians that these enemies have their minds "on earthly things. But our citizenship is in heaven" (Philippians 3:19-20).

Our understanding of this eternal destination leads to several additional observations about leadership. For example, it enables the leader to *endure hardship* of many kinds. Paul and Peter certainly knew hardship for the cause of the Gospel. Further, it enables the leader to be *freed from a preoccupation with pursuing material gain.* Paul's words to Timothy are particularly instructive:

> But godliness with contentment is great gain. For we brought nothing into the world, and we can take nothing out of it. But if we have food and clothing, we will be content with that. People who want to get rich fall into temptation and a trap and into many foolish and harmful desires that plunge men into ruin and destruction. . . . But you, man of God, flee from all of this and pursue righteousness, godliness, faith, love, endurance and gentleness. . . . Command those who are rich in this present world not to be arrogant nor to put their hope in wealth, which is so uncertain, but to put their hope in God, who richly provides us with everything for our enjoyment. Command them to do good, to be rich in good deeds, and to be generous and willing to share (1 Timothy 6:6-9, 11, 17-18).

Following Paul's counsel frees the leader from having to make job-related decisions driven primarily by a personal desire for economic security. As Ron Cline, former educator now missionary leader, noted in a church missions conference, we tend to get sidetracked from God in our pursuit to collect more "stuff." Yet we know the kingdom does not consist of the collection of more "stuff." Further, our preoccupation with the kingdom frees us to make organizational decisions which we believe are in keeping with that kingdom. We are thus freed from the reluctance to make decisions which may threaten our job security. It is God, after all, who supplies all our needs.

There is a *sixth* observation, or group of observations, and I mention these only briefly. *Self-control is necessary* for leaders. Paul's letter to Titus repeatedly mentions the need for this character quality. Peter discusses the same priority in 1 Peter 1:13 and 4:7. There are numerous times in leadership roles where one is tempted to lose control, to really "blow away" someone. Spirit-controlled leaders counter with self-control, gentleness, and love. Tough teaching, but necessary.

Both Peter and Paul also saw *the need for confrontation.* Both confronted each other and many others in the course of their leadership. (I have discussed this issue more fully in my previous book.) They also knew how to *say thank you* and to *express appreciation to others* for both good work done and for personal expressions or good deeds extended to them. Paul's example recorded in Philippians 4:10, 14 is but one such instance. Affirmation and gratitude are important elements in leading, both to people and to the Lord. All of us have a felt need for such encouragement.

I want to close this chapter by noting two additional observations that made both Paul and Peter effective leaders. Both *were continually open to new ideas from the Lord.* Had Paul remained steeped in his original understanding that only the Jews belonged to God, he would not have known ministry to the Gentiles. Had Peter been disobedient to the "kill and eat" vision, he would not have known the joy of seeing Gentiles respond to the Gospel. Their obedience led them into previously uncharted waters of fruitful ministry. Like them, we need to stand ready to respond to new ideas and possibly new directions as we faithfully follow the leadership of the Spirit in our lives.

Finally, both had learned to *be positive in their leadership,* even when matters could be viewed by others as extremely negative or troublesome. Peter told his readers to *"rejoice,* though now for a little while you may have to suffer grief in all kinds of trials. . . . If you suffer as a Christian, do not be ashamed, but *praise God* that you bear that name" (1 Peter 1:6; 4:16, emphasis mine). One of Paul's great teachings on being positive is found in Philippians 4:8: "Finally, brothers, *whatever* is .true, *whatever* is noble, *whatever* is right, *whatever* is pure, *whatever* is lovely, *whatever* is admirable—if *anything* is excellent or praiseworthy—think about such things" (emphasis mine).

Every leader knows the reality of dealing with the negatives—the burdens and frustrations, the disappointments and failures—of leadership. But into the middle of all of those troubling events march Peter and Paul, telling us to "rejoice, praise God, be thankful in all things, and think positive." That kind of thinking is possible only because we know intimately the great God whom we serve, who is able to sustain and keep us through incredible adversity. Being positive is possible because of *who* we serve.

At the close of his long and difficult life, during which he faithfully served Christ to the end, Paul was able to express this note of incredible joy. Everyone who leads and follows can aspire to this same kind of faithfulness in leadership for the cause of the kingdom:

> The time has come for my departure. I have fought the good fight, I have finished the race, I have kept the faith. Now there is in store for me the crown of righteousness, which the Lord, the righteous Judge, will award to me on that day—and not only to me, but also to all who have longed for His appearing (2 Timothy 4:6-8).

Amen!

QUESTIONS FOR FURTHER THOUGHT AND DISCUSSION

1. Do you ever get a sense that Paul, as a leader, was or was not a team player? In what ways?
2. Would Paul insist that people must always be obedient to their leaders? Why or why not?

3. In your opinion, would Paul welcome women to positions of leadership? Why or why not?
4. How do you explain Paul's "falling out" with Barnabas over his cousin John Mark? (see Acts 15:36-41) Was Paul giving John Mark a standard of perfection that Paul himself failed to meet? Is there evidence to suggest that John Mark and Paul were eventually reconciled?
5. Do you sense that Peter and Paul were close friends or merely colleagues? On what basis do you draw your conclusions?
6. Do we get any hints about the kind of organizational structure that Peter and Paul would favor? Would they be the same or different? Or is that something they would even care about?
7. Would either Paul or Peter favor accountability in leadership? In what ways?

CONCLUSION

Leadership has at least two dimensions. First, it has an *upside-down dimension.* When the prevailing forces around me argue that I need to exert my power and "be the leader" (of course there is an element of truth to this admonition), I must also remember the teachings of Jesus. I must learn to exercise leadership by learning how to be a follower, a follower of Christ and also of the people I lead. I am not to lord my leadership over others. I am not to seek always to be first. I am not to be the "boss." Jesus is the one to be served and I am always to be the servant.

When Jesus in Mark 10:44 tells us to be the "slave of all," He "summarily removes any notion of leadership among his disciples which retains the faintest whiff of either status or domination."[1] As Stevens puts the matter, "We choose the way of hierarchy, of control, either overtly or covertly. He [Christ] chose the way of downward mobility."[2] We want to lead in a top-down manner. He wants us to lead upside down.

The degree to which I learn to follow Christ and reflect the qualities of His life in my leading and following will do much to determine my effectiveness in leadership. Much of what I wrote in *The Other Side of Leadership* was targeted in the direction of helping us understand better this *upside-down* dimension of leadership. One more biblical example will serve again to illustrate this concept.

In 1 Chronicles 13:1-4, the people were intent on making David king. The text notes that David conferred with each of his leaders and then "with the whole assembly of Israel." He shared his idea of what should happen with the people, beginning his presentation to them this way: "If it seems good to you and if it is the will of the Lord." In other words, David promised to provide direction subject to *the sense of the people* and, more importantly, to *the will of the Lord.* The people responded to David in this manner: "The whole assembly agreed to do this, because it seemed right to the people." This dual concern, one that earnestly and genuinely solicits the reactions and counsel of the people, on the one hand, and makes sure that the action contemplated is consistent with the will of God, on the other, is the essence of leading and following.

A primary focus of this book, however, has been on this second dimension of leadership, the *inside-out dimension.* We've seen again and again in Scripture that, before one is qualified for leadership, the Lord is vitally concerned that the person's heart reflect God-honoring qualities.

I remain persuaded that the inner side of leadership is critically important for those who name the name of Christ, whether leading in the context of a Christian organization or in a secular one. If "being" precedes "doing," and I am convinced that is the case, then wherever God calls me to serve, I need to display in both my personal and my organizational actions what He calls me to *be* as a Christian. Paul's instructions in Galatians 6:10 help me understand this better: "Therefore, as we have opportunity, let us do good to all people, especially to those who belong to the family of believers."

The quality of my leadership will be largely determined by the attention I pay to this inner side of leadership. In this domain I must honestly and regularly grapple with such questions as: How is my walk with the Lord? How is my relationship with my covenant partner in marriage? What about my children? What is the quality of my devotional life? My prayer life?

Interestingly, many if not all of these areas are seldom seen by the public. People may see my family in church; they may hear me or my wife speak at a meeting; they may see our children in other isolated roles. Yet it is the family who knows best what the "leader" is really like. Of course God knows as well. To be sure, the inner qualities of character are ultimately seen in some form by a watching world as it observes the leader as a leader. But if the right kinds of qualities are missing, the wrong kinds of things will happen in leadership. So, before I lead, I must be a follower of Christ. I must know Him and His resurrection power and then let Him, through the Holy Spirit, empower me and transform the inner side of my leadership. Where He leads, I must follow.

That Paul was concerned about this inner dimension is amply illustrated in many of his New Testament writings. One of my favorites is Ephesians 3:16-21:

> I pray that out of His glorious riches *He may strengthen you with power* through His Spirit *in your inner being*, so that Christ may dwell in your hearts through faith. And *I pray that you*, being rooted and established in love, *may have power*, together with all the saints, *to grasp how wide and long and high and deep is the love of Christ*, and to know this love that surpasses knowledge—that you may be filled to the measure of all the fullness of God. Now to Him who is able to do immeasurably more than all we ask or imagine, according to His power that is at work within us, to Him be glory in the church and in Jesus Christ throughout all generations, for ever and ever! Amen (emphasis mine).

Among other things, Paul was concerned about the Spirit's empowerment of his readers' inner beings; he was concerned that they would have understanding in order to grasp the incredible dimensions of Christ's love. These truths in themselves, put into practice, would be enough to transform an organization and its leadership. But then Paul provides the incredible thought that Christ, through His power that is at work in us, within our inner being, is able to do *"immeasurably more than all we ask or imagine."* What encouragement for those who desire faithfulness in their service for Christ. Presumably this includes leaders.

While reading books on leadership can help in leading, while taking coursework can add a depth of understanding about leadership, we must continually be taught by and learn from the One who tells us to follow—Jesus, the Master Leader. As leaders, we need to hear afresh His call to follow Him: "Come to Me, all you who are weary and burdened, and I will give you rest. Take My yoke upon you and *learn* from Me, for I am gentle and humble in heart, and you will find rest for your souls. For My yoke is easy and My burden is light" (Matthew 11:28-30, emphasis mine). These are not the words of a commander or boss. These are the gracious words of One who gave His life for us, of One who learned obedience, of One who did the bidding of His Father and became a servant. This is inside-out leading at its very best.

Henri Nouwen in his books *The Wounded Healer* and *In the Name of Jesus*[3] perceptively comments on the importance of this inside-out dimension of leadership. He notes, for instance, *that our preoccupation with busyness tends to hide our real need, to know Jesus better.* Sometimes we pretend that our busyness is job-related. But many times honesty compels us to admit that busyness may only be a mask to cover up our need to address our innermost thoughts. Nouwen recounts the story of a colleague who with despair was recounting "his hectic daily schedule—religious services, classroom teaching, luncheon and dinner engagements, and organizational meetings." According to Nouwen, this colleague observed the following about his own busyness: "I guess I am busy in order to avoid a painful self-concentration."[4] Might it be that our busyness in leadership is sometimes only a disguised attempt to avoid knowing who we really are as leaders?

Nouwen further observes that *our capacity to focus on our inner side actually gives us freedom to lead.* (The reverse, unfortunately, is probably also true.) Knowing who we are on the inside helps us empower others. Says Nouwen: "When we have found the anchor places for our lives in our own center, we can be free to let others enter the space created for them."[5] He even goes so far as to make the intriguing observation that one of the roles for future leaders is to be "articulators of *inner* events" (emphasis mine). Yet he notes that many leaders are unprepared for this important leadership role: "It is a painful fact indeed to realize how poorly prepared most Christian leaders prove to be when they are invited to be spiritual leaders in the true sense. Most of them are used to thinking in terms of large-scale organization, getting people together in churches, schools and hospitals, and running the show as a circus director. They have become unfamiliar with, and even somewhat afraid of, the deep and significant movements of the Spirit."[6]

We learn yet a further principle of inner leading from Nouwen, and it is this: *Centering on the inner side of leadership and being preoccupied with Christ permits us to be persons of hope.* Because of our relationship with Christ, we not only have an inner hope, but we also have hope in the future and in other people:

> A Christian leader is not a leader because he announces a new idea and tries to convince others of its worth; he is a leader because he faces the world with eyes full of expectation, with the expertise to take away the veil that covers . . . hidden potential.[7]

> A Christian leader is a man of hope whose strength in the final analysis is based neither on self-confidence derived from his personality, nor on specific expectations for the future, but on a promise given to him. . . . Leadership . . . is not called Christian because it is permeated with optimism against all the odds of life, but because it is grounded in the historic Christ-event.[8]

When we identify as leaders with Christ and His suffering; when we understand His brokenness for us and experience His forgiveness to us; when we understand our own brokenness and inadequacies; then we are better able to recognize anew our need to lead others with this inside-out perspective.

Finally, Nouwen observes that the most important element and need for leaders and leadership is for us to be people of God, who are deeply in love with the Saviour: "If there is any focus that the Christian leader of the future will need, it is the discipline of dwelling in the presence of the One who keeps asking us, 'Do you love me?' 'Do you love me?' 'Do you love me?' "[9] Nouwen writes:

> It is not enough for the priests and ministers (executives,

teachers, etc.) of the future to be moral people, well-trained, eager to help their fellow humans, and able to respond creatively to the burning issues of their time. All of that is very valuable and important, but it is not the heart of Christian leadership. The central question is, are the leaders of the future truly men and women of God, people with an ardent desire to dwell in God's presence, to listen to God's voice, to look at God's beauty, to touch God's incarnate Word and to taste fully God's infinite goodness![10]

Our task, suggests Nouwen, is for leaders to be consumed by the Saviour's love, and to have His love impact and shape our leading and following. To paraphrase J.I. Packer, once we as leaders understand that our primary business in leading is to follow Him, that we are here "to know God," then our other problems and agenda in leadership "fall into place of their own accord."[11] We follow Him "so that every word spoken, every advice given, and every strategy developed can come from a heart that knows God intimately."[12]

To be sure, leaders lead and followers follow. There are also leaders who follow and followers who lead. In the same way there are power-hungry leaders who think leading is "bossing" and impressing people with "my" power, rather than *helping them through empowerment.* So too are there willy-nilly leaders who, while servants, never help anybody accomplish anything for the work and ministry of the kingdom. The call of this book is for *upside-down leaders who will lead from inside-out.* We know that indeed this is a paradox: "The paradox of Christian leadership is that the way *out* is the way *in*" (emphasis mine).[13]

To all who aspire to this kind of leadership, keep leading, keep following, keep leading, keep following, and keep leading . . . above all, *with a follower's heart* in love with Jesus.

I conclude with this slight modification of Jude 24-25:

To Him *who is able to keep you* [leaders and followers] *from falling* and to present you before His glorious presence *without fault* and with great joy—to the only God our Saviour be *glory, majesty, power and authority,* through Jesus Christ our Lord, before all ages, now and evermore! Amen.

ENDNOTES

Introduction
1. Bruce W. Jones, *Ministerial Leadership in a Managerial World* (Wheaton: Tyndale House Publishers, 1988), p. 61.
2. Bobb Biehl and James W. Hagelganz, *Praying* (Sisters, Ore.: Questar Publishers, Inc., 1989), pp. 12–13.

Chapter One
1. John Kotter, *The Leadership Factor* (New York: The Free Press, 1988), p. 124.
2. Robert Kelley, *The Wall Street Journal*, April 8, 1988.
3. William Willimon and Robert Wilson, *Rekindling the Flame* (Nashville: Abingdon Press, 1987), p. 109.
4. Calvin Miller, *Leadership* (Colorado Springs: NavPress, 1987), p. 7.
5. Henri Nouwen, *In the Name of Jesus* (New York: The Crossroad Publishing Company, 1989), p. 57.
6. Quoted in Habecker, *The Other Side of Leadership* (Wheaton: Victor Books, 1987), p. 217.
7. Robert Kelley, "In Praise of Followers," *Harvard Business Review* (November-December 1988), p. 146.
8. Robert Birnbaum, *Leadership and Followership: The Cybernetics of University Governance* (New York: National Center for Postsecondary Governance and Finance, Columbia University, 1987), p. 6.
9. Habecker, *The Other Side of Leadership*, p. 218.

10. "What Makes A Great Teacher," *The Bulletin*, July 18, 1989.
11. Ibid., pp. 46–52.
12. See Habecker, *The Other Side of Leadership*, pp. 85–88.
13. Ibid., pp. 60–72.

Chapter Two
1. Rebecca M. Pippert, *Hope Has Its Reasons* (San Francisco: Harper & Row, 1989), p. 5.
2. *The Abingdon Bible Commentary* (Nashville: Abingdon-Cokesbury Press, 1929), p. 1281.

Chapter Three
1. Frank Tillapaugh, *Unleashing Your Potential* (Ventura, Calif.: Regal Books, 1988), p. 191.
2. Kenneth Gangel, *Feeding and Leading* (Wheaton: Victor Books, 1989), p. 124.
3. Ibid., p. 31.
4. David L. McKenna, *Power to Follow, Grace to Lead* (Dallas: Word Books, 1989), p. 25.
5. J. Robert Clinton, *The Making of a Leader* (Colorado Springs: NavPress, 1988), p. 91.
6. Ibid., p. 255.
7. Ibid., p. 91
8. Wesley L. Duewel, *Ablaze for God* (Grand Rapids: Francis Asbury Press, 1989).
9. Ibid., p. 194.
10. Ibid., p. 195.
11. Ibid.
12. Arthur F. Miller and Ralph T. Mattson, *The Truth about You* (Old Tappan, N.J.: Fleming H. Revell, 1977).
13. Ibid., p. 16.
14. Ibid., p. 17.
15. Ibid., pp. 41–42.
16. Bruce W. Jones, *Ministerial Leadership in a Managerial World* (Wheaton: Tyndale House Publishers, 1988), p. 55. See in particular chapter three entitled "How Do We Use the Gifts?"
17. Ibid., p. 57.
18. Ibid., pp. 58–62.

19. Ibid., pp. 62–67.
20. McKenna, *Power to Follow, Grace to Lead*, p. 16.

Chapter Four
1. Robert Bellah et al., *Habits of the Heart* (San Francisco: Harper & Row Publishers, 1985), pp. 129–130.
2. Earl Radmacher, *You and Your Thoughts* (Wheaton: Tyndale House Publishers, 1977).
3. Ron Blue, *Master Your Money* (Nashville: Thomas Nelson Publishers, 1986), p. 19.
4. Walter Wangerin Jr., *As For Me and My House* (Nashville: Thomas Nelson, 1987), p. 251.

Chapter Six
1. Quoted in "Tyranny of the Urgent" in *Growing Strong in God's Family* (Colorado Springs: NavPress, 1987), pp. 21–22.
2. Quoted in Wesley L. Duewel, *Ablaze for God* (Grand Rapids: Francis Asbury Press, 1989), pp. 211, 213.
3. Ibid., p. 170.
4. Ibid., pp. 182, 184.
5. Ibid., pp. 211–212.
6. Richard J. Foster, *Celebration of Discipline* (San Francisco: Harper & Row, 1978), p. 30.
7. Ibid., p. 31.
8. Ibid.
9. Henri Nouwen, *The Wounded Healer* (Garden City, N.Y.: Image Books, 1979), p. 47.
10. Duewel, *Ablaze for God*, p. 170.
11. James Houston, *The Transforming Friendship* (Batavia, Ill.: Lion Publishing, 1989), p. 16.
12. Ibid.
13. Quoted in *Growing Strong in God's Family*, pp. 30, 32.
14. Bobb Biehl and James W. Hagelganz, *Praying* (Sisters, Ore.: Questar Publishers, Inc., 1989), p. 12.
15. Ibid., p. 15.
16. Ibid., p. 18.
17. Houston, *The Transforming Friendship*, p. 25.
18. Jerry Bridges, *The Practice of Godliness* (Colorado Springs: NavPress, 1983), p. 18.
19. Houston, *The Transforming Friendship*, p. 17.

20. Ibid., p. 14.
21. Ibid., p. 19.
22. *The Abingdon Bible Commentary* (Nashville: Abingdon-Cokesbury Press, 1929), p. 965.
23. Calvin Miller, *Leadership* (Colorado Springs: NavPress, 1987), p. 41.
24. *Abingdon Bible Commentary*, p. 965.
25. Ibid.
26. Biehl and Hagelganz, *Praying*, p. 16.
27. Cheryl Biehl, *Scriptural Meditation* (Sisters, Ore.: Questar Publications, Inc., 1989), p. 73.
28. Duewel, *Ablaze for God*, p. 212.
29. Ibid., p. 213.

Chapter Seven
1. John Gardner, *Self-Renewal* (San Francisco: Harper & Row, 1964), pp. 9–11.
2. John Kotter, *The Leadership Factor* (New York: The Free Press, 1988) p. 28.
3. Ibid., pp. 29–30.
4. Manfred F.R. Kets de Vries, *Prisoners of Leadership* (New York: John Wiley & Sons, 1989), p. iv.
5. Wesley L. Duewel, *Ablaze for God* (Grand Rapids: Francis Asbury Press, 1989), p. 231.

Chapter Eight
1. John Gardner, *Self-Renewal* (San Francisco: Harper & Row, 1964), p. 11.
2. John White and Ken Blue, *Healing the Wounded* (Downers Grove, Ill.: InterVarsity Press, 1985), pp. 165–179.
3. Ibid., pp. 167, 169, 200.
4. Gordon MacDonald, *Rebuilding Your Broken World* (Nashville: Oliver Nelson, 1988), p. 52.
5. Henri Nouwen, *In the Name of Jesus* (New York: The Crossroad Publishing Company, 1989), p. 24.
6. Kyle McQuillen in "College Park Newsette " September 1989, p. 1.

Chapter Nine
1. Frank Tillapaugh, *Unleashing the Church* (Ventura, Calif.: Regal Books, 1982), p. 124.

2. Ibid., p. 76.
3. Ibid., p. 123.
4. Ibid., p. 77.
5. William Willimon and Robert Wilson, *Rekindling the Flame* (Nashville: Abingdon Press, 1987), p. 104.
6. Ibid., p. 104.
7. Ibid., p. 112.
8. Ibid., pp. 98–101.
9. Tillapaugh, *Unleashing the Church*, p. 103.
10. Ibid.
11. Robert Bellah, *Habits of the Heart* (San Francisco: Harper & Row Publishers, 1985), p. 241.
12. Tillapaugh, *Unleashing the Church*, p. 127.
13. Ibid., p. 126.

Chapter Eleven
1. Joyce Landorf, *Joseph* (Old Tappan, N.J.: Fleming H. Revell, 1979), p. 241.
2. Calvin Miller, *Leadership* (Colorado Springs: NavPress, 1987), p. 42.
3. Landorf, *Joseph*, p. 284.
4. Miller, *Leadership*, p. 94.
5. Landorf, *Joseph*, p. 301.
6. Ibid., p. 308.
7. *Eerdman's Handbook to the Bible* (Grand Rapids: William B. Eerdmans Publishing Company, 1973), p. 430.

Chapter Twelve
1. John Pollock, *The Apostle* (Wheaton: Victor Books, 1985).
2. Ibid., p. 14.
3. Ibid., p. 15.
4. Ibid., p. 16.
5. Ibid.
6. Ibid., p. 15.
7. Ibid., p. 16
8. Ibid., p. 17.
9. Ibid.
10. Ibid.
11. Ibid., p. 18.
12. Ibid.

13. Ibid.
14. Ibid., p. 19.
15. Ibid., p. 19, 21.
16. Ibid., p. 25.
17. Ibid., p. 31.
18. Ibid., p. 33.
19. Ibid., p. 43.
20. Ibid., p. 307.
21. Ibid.
22. Rebecca M. Pippert, *Hope Has Its Reasons* (San Francisco: Harper & Row, 1989), p. 11.
23. Ibid., p. 14.
24. Ibid.
25. Henri Nouwen, *In the Name of Jesus* (New York: The Crossroad Publishing Company, 1989), p. 25.
26. Gordon MacDonald, *Rebuilding Your Broken World* (Nashville: Oliver Nelson, 1988).
27. James Houston, *The Transforming Friendship* (Batavia, Ill.: Lion Publishing, 1989), pp. 228–33.

Conclusion

1. David Prior, *Jesus and Power* (Downers Grove, Ill.: InterVarsity Press, 1987), p. 37.
2. Paul Stevens, *Marriage Spirituality* (Downers Grove, Ill.: InterVarsity Press, 1989), p. 140.
3. Henri Nouwen, *The Wounded Healer* (Garden City, N.Y.: Image Books, 1979) and *In the Name of Jesus* (New York: The Crossroad Publishing Company, 1989).
4. Nouwen, *The Wounded Healer*, p. 90.
5. Ibid., p. 91.
6. Ibid., p. 37–38.
7. Ibid., p. 75.
8. Ibid., p. 76.
9. Henri Nouwen, *In the Name of Jesus*, p. 28.
10. Ibid., pp. 29–30.
11. J.I. Packer, *Knowing God* (Downers Grove, Ill. InterVarsity Press, 1973), p. 29.
12. Nouwen, *In the Name of Jesus*, p. 30.
13. Nouwen, *The Wounded Healer*, p. 77.